The Islamism Debate

edited by
Martin Kramer

DAYAN CENTER PAPERS 120

The Moshe Dayan Center for Middle Eastern and African Studies seeks to contribute by research, documentation, and publication to the study and understanding of the modern history and current affairs of the Middle East and Africa. The Center is part of the Aranne School of History and the Lester and Sally Entin Faculty of Humanities at Tel Aviv University.

The Dayan Center Papers are monographs, collections of articles, and conference proceedings resulting from research done by the Center's fellows, associates, and guests. The series is a continuation of the Center's *Occasional Papers* series, published since 1970, and is edited by Ami Ayalon, a senior research associate at the Moshe Dayan Center.

The Dayan Center Papers are published by the Moshe Dayan Center and distributed worldwide by Syracuse University Press, 1600 Jamesville Avenue, Syracuse, NY 13244-5160; and in Israel by the Publications Department, the Moshe Dayan Center for Middle Eastern and African Studies, Tel Aviv University, Ramat Aviv 69978.

The Islamism Debate

edited by
Martin Kramer

with contributions by

Daniel Brumberg
François Burgat
Graham E. Fuller
Martin Kramer
Ann Elizabeth Mayer
Daniel Pipes
Olivier Roy
Robert Satloff
Claire Spencer

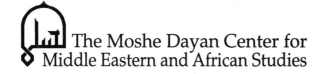 The Moshe Dayan Center for
Middle Eastern and African Studies

Tel Aviv University

Cover photograph: An Islamist demonstration in Cairo, 1 December 1993,
T. Hartwell/Sygma

Copyright © 1997 Tel Aviv University

ISBN: 965-224-024-9

Design: Ruth Beth-Or
Production: Elena Lesnick

Contents

Preface

In the mass of writings about Islamism, the intellectual battle lines have been drawn. Entire books argue this view or that; conferences are convened to promote one approach or another. The result is that there is no one volume where the interested reader can find all sides of the debate argued fully and fairly. *The Islamism Debate* is meant to fill that vacuum.

In these pages, nine of the leading protagonists in this debate, from the United States, France, Britain, and Israel, argue their cases with varying combinations of evidence, analysis, and polemic. Is Islamism driven by religious fervor, social protest, or nationalist xenophobia? Is the rise of Islamism a threat to stability, tolerance, and order? Or is it the first step towards reform, participation, and democratization? Does repression of Islamists radicalize them or tame them? Are Islamists in power guided by their ideals or their interests? Should the governments of the West base their policy on human rights or *realpolitik*? Does Islamism have the momentum to remake the future, or is it a rearguard action that is already failing? These are just some of the questions debated by the contributors to this volume. The reader is invited to weigh the evidence, compare the approaches, and reach his or her own conclusions.

The participants in this volume presented their views at a conference held by the Moshe Dayan Center for Middle Eastern and African Studies, convened at Tel Aviv University in March 1996. The conference met at a difficult time in Israel's own experience of Islamism, in the aftermath of a wave of Hamas "self-martyrdom" bombings and on the eve of Israel's "Operation Grapes of Wrath" against Hizbullah in Lebanon. Despite these local concerns, the participants were urged to conduct their debate within the largest possible frame of reference, with an emphasis on the Middle East and North Africa. To convey something of the spirit of the debate, a less formal style of writing has been encouraged, and parts of the discussion have been included. The tyranny of the clock made it impossible to discuss every presentation, and the absence of an appended discussion usually means that it took place over lunch or dinner and so, alas, off the record. I have also included one presentation not delivered at the conference: my own. My contribution was first delivered as the annual Goldman Lecture at Georgetown University in April 1995, and it appears here in revised form.

Many hands helped to make the conference a success. The conference enjoyed the support of the late Prime Minister Yitzhak Rabin, who authorized the necessary funding shortly before his assassination. Mr. Eitan Haber, Prof. Itamar Rabinovich, and Mr. Haim Israeli mediated between the Center and the Prime Minister. The United States Information Service in Tel Aviv also contributed to the funding of the conference. Then-Prime Minister Shimon Peres graciously consented to open the conference, and engaged participants in a lively exchange of questions and answers. Ms. Amira Margalith, my administrative assistant, once again acquitted herself brilliantly as a master of conference planning and logistics. Ms. Elena Lesnick saw this volume through the Center's own press. Each and every one of these contributions was vital to placing this volume in the reader's hands, and I am grateful for them all.

Martin Kramer

Are Islamists For or Against Democracy?

Against, maintains Daniel Brumberg: most Islamists are in thrall to authoritarian ideas about government, and the rest hedge their grudging acceptance of pluralism. For, says François Burgat: Islamists themselves are the prime victims of authoritarianism, and they represent the will of the people.

Rhetoric and Strategy:
Islamic Movements and Democracy
in the Middle East

Daniel Brumberg

We want the FLN to last, to be powerful so that it can...help us to make Algeria...strong. We want a strong front...not to be faced by the former corrupt, weak party. This opposition should strengthen the system of multi-party participation....The lion does not like to face himself...a lion needs someone to endanger him, to activate...his attention. We hope that the FLN will regain power and will stay a part of Algeria. There is nothing wrong with sharing power so long as power is for all the people.

The above statement was made by Abbasi Madani in the summer of 1990. At the time, he was the leader of Algeria's Islamic Salvation Front (FIS), a mass Islamic party which had recently prevailed over the National Liberation Front (FLN) in municipal and local elections. The observer of Middle East politics might interpret this statement as proof of FIS's commitment to pluralistic democracy. Yet how do we know when Islamists are genuinely supporting democracy or are merely engaging in tactics? Indeed, does this distinction matter at all in terms of the process of political liberalization—a process which in recent years has unfolded in some quarters of the Arab world?

Some would argue that political rhetoric of Islamists is of little consequence, that "discourse is just discourse." Still others demure in the opposite direction, equating the advocacy of a supposedly authentic "Islamic democracy" with the creation of democracy itself. I intend to argue that Islamic political rhetoric does matter in one specific sense: it is an integral part of political strategies which influence the perceptions and actions of ruling and opposition elites. Certain forms of political rhetoric facilitate the efforts of reformers to promote political openings, while other

Daniel Brumberg is assistant professor of government at Georgetown University.

kinds only reinforce elites opposed to reform. "Reformist fundamental-ist rhetoric," I argue, presents a particularly complex challenge. Precisely because it is based on a pragmatic utilitarianism that sees politics as a vehicle for establishing the "ethical state," Islamists can use reformist rhetoric to win allies within regimes and society. But because its ultimate goal is a unified Islamic state, reformist fundamentalism—combined with the use of what I call "tactical modernism"—presents a strategic threat that undermines the efforts of Arab political reformers while strengthen-ing the hand of hard-liners.

To make this case, I will begin by evaluating the revival of text-based studies of Islamic notions of democracy. Despite their apparent empha-sis on diversity, these studies often place different forms of Islamic ideol-ogy under one generalized rubric, thus echoing the very conceptual monism they strive to transcend. The alternative to textual idealism, I argue, is a sociological analysis of different Islamic ideologies that high-lights when these ideologies and those who espouse them promote or block political reform. Having sketched out this alternative, I use it to trace the course of political openings in Egypt and Algeria.

Arab Critics of Textual Idealism

The study of Islamic ideas or discourse is back in vogue. The current wave harks back to, but rarely matches, the pioneering studies of H.A.R. Gibb and Albert Hourani. It does so by examining the efforts of contemporary Muslims to reinterpret Islamic ideas in a liberal or pluralist light.[1] This revival of traditional scholarship requires the scrutiny of articles, books, and speeches, a much maligned art whose revival represents a *potentially* welcome development. After all, it wasn't so long ago that one writer—echoing the chilling effect of Edward Said's *Orientalism*—declared that "one may well be damned as soon as one mentions 'Islam' at all."[2] Bow-ing to the dominant canon of the times, he concluded that "it is more useful...to think about Muslims than to think about Islam."[3] Such think-ing, Leonard Binder later noted, suggests that one can speak about Mus-lims without ascribing any positive content to Islam itself—as if idea and action operate in separate realms instead of upon each other.[4]

It is precisely this link between intellectual and material forces that demands the study of ideas. Left in a vacuum, the pure study of ideas entails risks. For example, most of the recent studies of Islamic notions of democracy rarely provide an analytical yardstick by which to evaluate the link between ideas and political context. Their message seems to be that in the Islamic world, political problems are resolved at the level of doctrines that evoke the intrinsic fundamentals of Islamic "identity." Thus if we want to study democracy, the place to look is in "Islamic" notions of democracy; if we are looking for pluralism and notions of citizenship, then we have to look at efforts to revise the concept of *dhimma* or the *umma*.[5]

That such methodologies aim to show the adaptability (instead of rigidity) of Islamic norms does not necessarily represent an advance over what has been called "bad" Orientalism.[6] As Aziz Al-Azmeh notes, taken to extremes, "benign...neo-orientalism" suggests a "relativism...of mutual legitimacy (that) masquerades as a form of...understanding," an approach which sees "quotidian banalities as epoch-making and marking the boundaries of a chimerical cultural ego."[7]

By "banalities" Azmeh means ideology. Muslim activists may feel that their renderings of Islamic doctrine conform with the unchanging fundamentals of a true "Golden Age." But Azmeh argues that such renderings are not "truth" but are instead ideological formulations which rip events out of history in order to render political platforms sacred or "authentic." Islamic fundamentalists may be forgiven for not being aware of the subjectiveness of their ideas. But Western scholars, Azmeh insists, must recognize Islamist ideology as ideology—lest they confuse their categories of analysis with those of the Islamists themselves.

Paradoxically, some who warn vociferously of the dangers of imposing an artificial unity on the diversity of Islamic movements fall into the snare of conceptual monism that Azmeh warns against. For example, two prominent scholars assert that "Muslims unanimously agree on the unity of God as the central concept of Islamic faith, tradition and practice" and that this belief forms the basis of an "Islamic democracy" under whose umbrella, the authors argue, dwell thinkers as disparate as Abul A'la Mawdudi, Fazlur Rahman, and Muhammad Baqir al-Sadr. Similarly, in a recent article a Western journalist repeated the familiar warning that "politicized Islam is not a monolith," only to argue that the Islamic world is undergoing a "reformation" comparable to the Protestant Reformation.[8] The leaders of this reformation can be identified *by their advocacy of an idea*, namely that "Islam's tenets can be interpreted to accommodate and even encourage pluralism."[9] On this sole criterion the author then places the Iranian philosopher Abdolkarim Sorush and the Tunisian Islamist Rashid al-Ghannushi under the supposedly discriminating umbrella of the "Islamic Reformation"!

Asked to comment on the article, a former ally of Ghannushi, Muhammad al-Hashimi Hamdi, suggested "that there is a problem." The author, he argues,

> is mostly interested in Muslims who, in effect speak her mind back to her in terms that she finds familiar, and who reassure her of the supremacy of her own Western values. Ghannushi fits this role perfectly. As an exiled politician seeking support from Western circles...his strategy has been to play the "democratic card."

The Moroccan philosopher Abdou Filali Ansari pursues a similar line of argument but gives it greater conceptual depth. The article, he states, "raises troubling questions." To begin with, "how and why did the author choose her two subjects?" While both "accept Islam as a point of reference...there is...an important difference masked by their apparent allegiance to the same flag." That difference, he argues, comes down to this: "For Ghannushi, the principal question is always how to free the community from backwardness and dependence on 'the other.' However significant his concessions in favor of democracy...the community—not the individual—remains...the ultimate...objective. Democracy and freedom...are tools for raising the community of Muslims to the level of power and efficiency that Western nations currently enjoy." In contrast, Ansari argues,

> Sorush is not interested in showing Muslims how to achieve a more advantageous competitive position in the struggle with "the other." For him, the main adversary dwells within Muslims themselves...The urgent task is...to free Muslims from Islam understood as a social and historical heritage...Sorush wants to make follow-

ers of Islam more inwardly Muslim by enabling them to adopt piety based on free adherence.

Thus, Ansari concludes, "if we adopt the comparison with what happened in Christendom, the dividing line between Sorush and Ghannushi is more or less equivalent to the one that separated the Reformation from the Counter Reformation."

Ansari's point is conceptual: for him, there are three critical factors that distinguish fundamentalist from liberal modernist ideology. First, genuine (or what I call "strategic") modernists are not interested in reinterpreting Islam as a means of pursuing a "civilizational" strategy vis-à-vis the West. Second, genuine modernists reject subordinating individual rights to community rights, thereby imposing notions of community that, as Ansari puts it, enforce "custom, habit and conformism." Finally, Ansari argues that political efficacy of modernism depends on what political scientists would call "sequences of political development." He notes that "in the Muslim world, secularization is preceding religious reformation— a reversal of the European experience in which secularization was more or less a consequence of such reformation." Obviously, history cannot be repeated twice (even as farce!), and Ansari's point seems to be that Islamic liberalism will prevail only when its adherents make a clear-cut strategic case for secularism.

Democracy Without Democrats? Rationality Without Ideology?

Ansari's critique reminds us that a persuasive account of the role that Islamic political rhetoric plays in democratic reform requires two things. First, we must abandon ahistorical notions of "Islamic democracy" or "Islamic Reformation" in favor of sociological studies of Islamic ideologies and movements. Second, we must embed these studies in *a theory of democratic change* that suggests which Islamic ideologies advance or hinder democratization, and delineates under what circumstances their espousal affects the course of political reform.

Here I can only sketch the barest of answers to these two questions. Let me begin by setting out a theory of democratic reform. To do so, I propose adopting a modified version of the instrumentalist "transitions" paradigm that has become so popular in recent years. This holds that the adoption of democracy is the result of a pragmatic calculation by which rulers and opposition forces embrace democracy as a means of addressing the economic and social crises of failed authoritarian regimes. Democratic transitions are thus a form of domestic peacemaking between ideological enemies. Confronted by repeated failure, antagonists forge power-sharing arrangements or "democratic bargains" that protect the minimal interests of each side. In practice, this means that to gain admission to the democratic game, opposition forces must demonstrate that they will *not* use democracy as a tool for liquidating every vestige of the ruling elite's political or financial power.[10]

One of the assumptions of instrumentalist transitions theory is that "rational" rather than philosophical, ethical or even ideological calculations produce what one writer has aptly called "democracy without democrats."[11] However, the role of ideology cannot be dismissed by tautologies that define away the problem. I would argue that democratic bargains presuppose a learning process by which adversaries acquire a new conception of what makes a valid political community. We might have "democracy without democrats," but as President Nelson Mandela has shown so clearly in the case of South Africa, we cannot have power sharing unless elites at least implicitly embrace norms such as political pluralism as intrinsically valid ends. In short, we are compelled to return to ideology and its role in securing or hindering democratic bargains.

Since Islamic movements and ideologies figure prominently in the Middle East, we must ask whether all Islamists are equally prepared to embrace the norms of power sharing. Can their quest for an "Islamic state" be squared with the notion of a democratic bargain struck among ideological enemies? These questions cannot be usefully answered by placing Islamic ideologies under the category of "Islamic democracy." Instead, we must distinguish between different Islamic ideologies and assess their implications for the striking of democratic bargains. For my purposes, I identify four types of Islamist rhetoric.

Reformist fundamentalism posits an authoritarian concept of the community that calls for subordinating the rights of the individual to the ethical imperatives of the community. This vision is inspired by a utopian idealization of the early Islamic community, in which, as Hasan al-Banna wrote, "unity, in all its means and manifestations, pervaded this new-risen *umma*."[12] However, it would be misleading to over-emphasize the role played by the idealization of the first *umma*. Despite its apparent focus on the Sunna of the Prophet and his Companions, reformist fundamentalism is animated by a utilitarianism that views politics—and the state itself—merely as a vehicle for realizing the collective moral will.[13] This utopian utilitarianism has two roots, one quite old and the other more recent. On the one hand it finds inspiration partly in medieval Islamic political theory. According to this theory, "*siyasa* [politics] denotes absolutist management, the direction by reason of unreason...It is the management of natural disorder by the order of culture, and regal power is the ultimate state of culture in a natural word of man marked by a *bellum omnium contra omnes* which necessitates that establishment of power."[14] On the other hand, this utilitarianism is inspired by modern and distinctly *secular* conceptions of mass politics, concepts that view the state as the direct embodiment of a society's collective nature or general will. It is the echo of Rousseau more than verses of the Qur'an which resounds when Mawdudi writes that Islamic government "is constituted by the general will of the Muslims,"[15] or when Hasan al-Turabi argues that the "phrase 'Islamic state'...is a misnomer, [because]...the state is only the political dimension of the collective endeavor of Muslims."[16]

This utilitarian logic has significant implications for democracy in general and the striking of democratic bargains in particular. Because reformist fundamentalists believe that the state is "only the political expression of an Islamic society,"[17] and because they hold that a wide variety of political vessels can contain this society, they enthusiastically *embrace* "liberal" notions such as gradual political liberalization and strengthening civil society. Both are indispensable preludes to creating an Islamic state. This said, because their long-term strategic goal remains building a unified ethical order, and because ruling elites are well aware of this strategic vision, the reformists' accommodationist logic cannot be the basis of forging a "democratic bargain." On the contrary, the closer this logic comes to realizing its ultimate goal, the more it threatens the vital interests of ruling elites, thus hindering a transition to pluralist politics.

Militant fundamentalism rejects the notion of gradualism and instead demands the forced imposition of an Islamic state. Inspired by Sayyid Qutb's writings, militants argue that because all of society is in a state of pre-Islamic ignorance *(jahiliyya)*, Muslims cannot reform society "from within" without being corrupted by it. For the militants, the imposition of a new ethical order by revolutionary action will create the ethical man and not the other way around. This militancy clearly precludes the striking of a democratic bargain.

Strategic modernism advances a liberal democratic vision of the state. It explicitly rejects the notion of politics as means by which Muslims subordinate the rights of the individual to the collective imperatives of the ethical state. Echoing the ideas of Ali Abd al-Raziq, strategic modernists such as Laith Kubba and Abdolkarim Sorush argue that the state exists to protect the rights of Muslims to freely express their individual vision of Islam. This approach is acceptable to political reformers and thus its advocacy can further the prospects for a transition to democracy.

Tactical modernism entails the selective use of modernist themes to advance a fundamentalist agenda. In contrast to the above forms of Islamic ideology—which can take on organized political form—tactical modernism is a rhetorical device that reformists use to secure the support of social groups—such as the intelligentsia—that might otherwise not embrace the fundamentalist project. The implications of this latter point for democratic reform merit additional comment.

Tactical Modernism and Reformist Fundamentalism

Tactical modernism and reformist fundamentalism are closely linked. As I have already noted, the utilitarian nature of reformist fundamentalism is intrinsically suited to a gradualist program by which Islamists forge alliances with a variety of groups. To address their more orthodox followers, reformists will speak in fundamentalist terms, evoking notions of the primacy of the community, Islamic law and unity. To address potential allies in the professional middle class and intelligentsia who might not share these authoritarian values, reformists will integrate into their rhetoric ideas, themes and symbols drawn from the modernist repertoire. Both forms of Islamic rhetoric often coexist in the same text, speech or campaign pamphlet—even though they are distinct from one another. That is why those who examine Islamic discourse with an untrained eye can so easily confuse the appearance of modernism with the reality of fundamentalism.

Here are two examples of Islamist rhetoric that illuminate its "constructive ambiguity," as a colleague calls it. First, let us consider an excellent example of the ambiguities of reformist fundamentalism.

Ma'mun al-Hudaybi, the Egyptian Muslim Brother, was recently asked in an interview what the difference is between the Muslim Brethren of today and those of Hasan al-Banna's era. His reply: "There is one program, which has neither experienced change nor substitution. This is because Allah sanctions the following (*'abad*) of this program. The goals and the aims of this program are one—they are to gather people around truth, love, brotherhood, friendship, and compassion, in order to live in the framework of *shari'a*."[18] The interviewer pointed out to Hudaybi that in Hasan al-Banna's time, it was believed that multiparty politics was not Islamic, whereas Banna's successors believe that this system is in conformity with Islam. What was the catalyst that led to this change? Here is Hudaybi's response:

> Shaykh Hasan al-Banna announced several times that the Muslim Brethren do not pursue power and do not want to govern. Instead they are a call (*daw'a*), for man to embrace Islam as a way of life. Banna participated in Egypt's elections not as a means to gain power, but rather as a way of spreading the message...If Shaykh Hasan al-Banna went on record as supporting a party system (*hizbiyya*)...this was because of party strife rather than the acceptance of this system in principle. The Muslim Brethren today are of the same opinion as the Brethren of yesterday. They adhere to principled positions, based on the Qur'an and the Sunna...They are for pluralism and...the right to form parties, and for continuing to carry out that which adheres to the way of Allah—may He be praised—for He is the final authority.

What are we to make of such a statement? On the one hand, Hudaybi insists that the "Muslim Brethren today are of the same opinion as the Brethren of yesterday," noting that Hasan al-Banna ran in elections for pragmatic reasons, not because he accepted multiparty politics "in principle." On the other hand, he insists that the Brethren favor party pluralism and "do not pursue power." To the uninitiated, this statement can be interpreted in different ways—even positively. But I would argue that it accurately reflects the fusion of utopianism and utilitarianism that is at the heart of fundamentalist ideology. As Azmeh puts it, "Islamist political discourse always insists that the Islamic party is not a political party on a par with other political parties, but that it is distinguished by being consonant with [an] ontologically privileged history...It represents the element of continuity, and is therefore above and beyond political dissent."[19] Thus from Hudaybi's perspective, because the Brethren's mission is to "call man to embrace a way of life," it is perfectly consistent for them to reject multiparty politics one day and embrace it the other *since both forms of politics can serve the same ethical ends.* This trans-political view allows—*indeed calls for*—temporary alliances with secularists so long as it is understood that the Brethren represent a "truth" that sets them above mere politics. As Sayf al-Islam Hasan al-Banna—the son of the founder of the Brethren—recently put it when asked whether Islamists would cooperate with leftist parties: "Look, we do not ally with the left as a *party.*"[20]

Now let us consider an example of tactical modernism that is blended with fundamentalist themes. One of the favorite targets of this kind of Islamic ideology is Western academics. Addressing such an audience in 1982, Turabi advanced what appeared to be an Islamic modernist vision. The Islamic state, he insisted, "rules out all forms of absolutism," because "the caliph was freely elected by the people who thereby have precedence over him as a legal authority." Thus, Turabi explained, "it follows that an Islamic order...is essentially a form of representative democracy." But Turabi subtly balanced his evocation of modernist themes with concepts consonant with the authoritarian utilitarianism of reformist fundamentalism. "The phrase 'Islamic state'," he explained "is a misnomer. The state is only the political dimension of the collective endeavor of Muslims." In fact, he explained, the Qur'anic injunction of *shura* or consultation could *not* be equated with Western democracy. "In their mutual consultations, the citizens [of the Islamic state] work towards a consensus that unites them. The majority/minority pattern in politics is not an ideal one in Islam." Thus, he concluded, while "there is no legal bar to...different parties...an Islamic government should function more as a consensus-oriented system rather than a minority/majority system with political parties rigidly confronting each other."[21]

In short, whatever concessions Turabi made to Islamic modernism in his effort to appeal to a Western audience, he remained loyal to the premises of his fundamentalism—thus ensuring that his most loyal supporters would not accuse him of betraying the cause.

In a recent interview with Turabi, Al-Hashimi Hamdi noted that during a visit to the United States in 1992, several American academics argued that Turabi's rhetoric had become, as Hamdi put it, "more authoritarian (akthara shumuliyya), indeed that it supported a totalitarian system. Have your ideas changed since... you were the leader of the National Islamic Front, during the era of political pluralism, and if so why?" Turabi responded incredulously:

> Many of those academics had really never listened to me before. What is the Sudan for them when they talk about it, and who this Turabi they were listening to and talking about? When I was in America I only spoke...to a small number of American academics whose number didn't even total seven fingers, one hand....As for those who follow the case of the Sudan now, they do so because the Sudan has become a stark symbol of something that worries them. They don't know me well enough to compare my position today to my position before, they barely listened to me....Those who *were* listening to me...can testify to that point....Those who judge this government are hypocrites. There are many governments around the Sudan, and when we measure them according to the yardsticks of democracy and human rights we find that their record is worse than that of the Sudan.[22]

It is tempting to see in this response merely an effort to dodge the question. But Turabi is quite correct to assail the claim that his rhetoric had fundamentally changed. The problem, he correctly observed, is that most Americans "don't know me well enough to compare my position of today to my position of before," i.e. his critics were not sufficiently familiar with his rhetoric to reach such a simplistic conclusion. As for his 1992 meeting with American academics, the published transcripts of this meeting show that Turabi ultimately voiced his devotion to an authoritarian agenda. He did so repeatedly, as when he enthusiastically endorsed an alliance with Arab nationalists and Nasserists, the most candid advocates of populist authoritarianism in the Arab world. These groups, Turabi insisted, "are now gradually returning to the fold....The masses have abandoned them, so they have to join the people." This said, Turabi was careful to evoke the utilitarian themes that were central to his ideology: "We just seek to express our Islamic values," he reassured his hosts.

> I...have been advising...Islamic movements to exhaust all means of peaceful dialogue because Islam...is better expressed peacefully....Revolution...is...not the best *method* of promoting Islam. Islam is better brought about without revolution because (a) it's a religion and (b) we don't have a very clear picture of the model yet, and it's better that we implement it gradually so that we learn as we go along.[23]

The Dilemmas and Limits of Utilitarian Utopianism

It is worth noting that Turabi's hosts interpreted his pragmatism more in the light of John Dewey than Ibn Taymiyya. As one participant put it, "If I were to summarize what I think is Dr. Hasan's message, it is...that the Islamic movement in the Sudan and Islamist movements elsewhere are movements *in process*; that everything is not yet finished."[24]

In and of itself, this assessment was accurate. However, by its nature, the utilitarianism that animates fundamentalist ideology only values "process" as a means, rather than as an end in itself. Everything may indeed "not be finished" for weeks, months and even years. But if political reform threatens to liquidate ruling elites by creating that "order of culture," to use Azmeh's evocative expression, or if the dynamics of reform foreclose the creation of the ethical state, pragmatic gradualism will lose some or all of its effectiveness.

Both processes were evident in Egypt and Algeria, the two countries where reformist fundamentalists have posed the most serious challenge to the state. During a first stage of a political reform process, the leaders of Islamic organizations accentuated the utilitarian spirit of fundamentalist Islam, as well as the liberal symbols of Islamic modernism. They did so in effort to attract the support of three groups: reformists within ruling circles; the professional middle class intelligentsia; and Western observers (both official and unofficial). At the same time, Islamists addressed the social base of their movement—the urban lower middle classes—in the authoritarian language of mass redemption that is central to fundamentalist ideology. However, where this rhetorical strategy was successful, or at least where it won Islamists greater access to the political arena, it soon gave way to a second stage during which Islamists abandoned gradualism in favor of a more radical program.

This process was often accelerated by the "structural dilemma" in which mainstream Islamists found themselves. Although many appreciated the value of gradualism and argued for a long-term strategy of sinking institutional roots in society, their mass constituency—upon whom their power seemed to depend—clamored for more immediate action. Pushed from above by the state, and pulled from below by a mass social base whose borders with the mainstream groups were overlapping and ambiguous, mainstream fundamentalists altered between gradualist programs and ideologies, and more radical programs and ideologies. The resulting pattern of ideological zig-zagging alienated the gradualists' youthful followers while discrediting regime "soft-liners" like President Chadli Benjedid, who had argued for a policy of selective inclusion. As a result, the striking of pacts or "democratic bargains" did not take place. On the contrary, in Algeria and Egypt the ideological ambiguities and inconsistencies of mainstream Islamists strengthened the hands of the "eradicationists," i.e. those who argued for excluding both reformist and militant fundamentalists from the political arena. I will now examine how these processes unfolded, paying particular attention to their ideological dynamics.

Egypt

Following the assassination of Sadat and the emergence of what seemed at the time to be a relatively more open political system under President Mubarak, the leaders of Egypt's mainstream Muslim Brethren opted for a policy of gradualism. To gain the support of the middle class and the New Wafd Party, the Brethren invoked pragmatic themes of reformist

fundamentalism, adding a dash of tactical modernism where appropriate. Thus Brethren leader Umar Talmasani implied that for the Brethren,
democracy was a strategic choice: "Democracy...is not a slogan that is
raised but it is a platform of thinking and a style of life....There is nothing
easier than for tyrants to praise freedom...for the sake of cover and affa-
bility."[25] Indeed, Talmasani went as far as to claim that elections were "an
opportunity that God gives to all the parties—an opportunity in which
all parties [will] submit their useful plans."[26] Moreover, in an effort to calm
fears regarding the Brethren's position on Islamic law, the organization's
leaders agreed with the New Wafd Party that the existing constitutional
provisions regarding shari'a were sufficient. Finally, to address concerns
about minority rights, Talmasani adopted the modernist credo that, as
he put it, "the Egyptian Copts are 'People of the Book' and they have in
an Islamic society the same duties the Muslims shoulder."[27]

The use of such rhetoric was successful during the 1984 elections. In
their alliance with the Wafd, the Brethren were allotted ten of the fifty-
eight seats won by the New Wafd in the 1984 elections. In the ensuing
years they widened their support among professionals and among the
urban poor. In time, this trend lessened the utility of the alliance with the
Wafd. Thus, in advance of the May 1987 elections, the Brethren allied with
the Labor Socialist Party (LSP), a populist party with strong Islamic roots,
particularly among the student population. The Islamic Alliance enabled
the Brethren and/or their allies to increase their representation in the
parliament by a factor of seven. Having chalked up another victory, Brethren member Mustafa Mashhur admitted that the alliance with the New
Wafd was a "temporary cooperation for a specific operation."[28] Explaining why the Brethren had shifted, he stated that the LSP had not only
invited the Brethren to field more candidates; more importantly, it had
given the application of Islamic law much greater prominence.[29] Breaking with the organization's previous promises to adhere to the constitution, the Brethren's new leader Hamid Abu al-Nasr called for a purge.
Everything that was at variance with "the spirit of Islam and its lofty law,"
he declared, should be outlawed, while the government should make
"every state official...responsible for his personal behavior if it is contrary
to Islamic laws." To back up this policy, he called for the application of
Islamic penalties and for ensuring that all judges should be bound by
Islamic law.[30]

Not surprisingly, these radical statements precluded the forging of a democratic pact. Against a background of economic crisis, the expansion of the Brethren's base in professional associations, the increasingly frequent violent attacks by militant Islamists, and finally the Gulf war, the regime's previous policy of accommodation began to give way to a hardline approach.

Algeria

This tendency to move from accommodationist language to radical rhetoric was even more pronounced in Algeria, largely because the opportunities for political power were much more real and immediate there in comparison to Egypt. At the outset of the reform process, there was a clear division of ideological labor between the leader of the Islamic Salvation Front, Abbasi Madani, and his deputy, Ali Belhadj. The former adopted the gradualist themes of reformist fundamentalism and tactical modernism in an effort to pacify the intelligentsia and gain the support of President Chadli Benjedid—the one member of the ruling elite who seemed genuinely committed to a political opening. Meanwhile, Belhadj adhered to the ideology of militant fundamentalism, seeking the support of the urban poor. Indeed, he uncategorically threatened to deprive his ideological enemies of their civil rights by amending Algeria's new constitution:

> We were shocked...that Article 40 of the draft constitution did not establish any safeguards....If today, the Berberist expresses his ideas (s'exprime), if the communist expresses himself, as well as all the others, our country will become an arena for the confrontation of diverse ideologies which contradict our beliefs....A Muslim cannot permit the appearance of parties which contradict Islam....Article 40 must be completed with a provision that links multipartism to Islam. If not we will categorically reject it.[31]

Madani subsequently crafted his rhetoric to offer a more moderate vision to his followers. In an interview six months before the June 1990 municipal and local elections, he seemed to embrace modernist principles. "My brother, how can we not coexist...and how can we not complement each other and why do we not help each other, when God says: 'Help ye one another in righteousness and piety but help ye not one another in sin...and in disobeying the Prophet.'?"[32] Similarly, one week after the elections he asked, "Why is it necessary to have pluralism?...Because one must have...opposition. Pluralism is necessary for political development because we are not angels. We are right sometimes, and make mistakes other times....Therefore pluralism must be permitted."[33]

Madani not only attempted to reassure his potential secular allies of his intentions; he went out of his way to assure other Islamists. "We are Muslims, but we are not Islam itself," he stated. "We do not monopolize religion. Democracy...means pluralism, choice and freedom." However, within weeks of the FIS victory in the 1990 municipal and local elections, Madani abandoned his promises to respect pluralism. Denouncing a proposal by Shaykh Nahnah to establish an "Islamic Alliance," he insisted that "anyone who wants unity should join our ranks for the establishing of an Islamic state." He then focused his attacks on the parliament itself, which in the fall of 1990 proposed amendments to the electoral law that Madani claimed would undermine FIS's position in the polls. "The parliament," he told a rally in November, "is merely a means for dialogue, and it has become useless. The FIS will only respect...the people's will, namely the setting up of an Islamic state this year."[34]

It should be noted that prior to the 1990 elections, Madani had not proposed the creation of an Islamic state. Apologists for the FIS have argued that his change was provoked by the government's unilateral modifications of the electoral law. But this analysis misses the essential point. For Madani, the parliament was, as he put it, "merely a means." Once this tool no longer served as a vehicle for realizing the "people's will"—as incarnated solely by the FIS—Madani was ready to jettison the institution in favor an creating an Islamic state.

Some weeks prior to Madani's spring 1991 confrontation with the Algerian government, he taped an interview with a Los Angeles-based public relations firm. Evidently, the FIS had hired the firm to project a more positive image to Americans. But far from projecting a mild or pluralistic image of the FIS, the interview unwittingly demonstrated the intoxicating effects of FIS's victory in the 1990 elections.

Madani began by insisting that the municipal elections, as well as the upcoming parliamentary poll, would achieve the sole—and thus far aborted—aim of the Algerian revolution, namely the creation of an Islamic state. The riots of 1988 and the subsequent political liberalization, he claimed in pragmatic terms, provided a new opportunity to realize that dream. "We had two directions to take for change," he explained, "either through violent revolution or through dialogue. We have chosen dialogue. Based on that choice we agreed to enter the...political struggle....The FIS uses both the tactics of persuasion and competition—persuasion...to convince the Algerian of the message...and political competition to impose the rights of the Algerian people to exist under a government of their choice."[35]

Having elucidated the pragmatic foundations of FIS's approach to politics, he then explained FIS's concept of democracy. "Democracy in Algeria cannot be given the same philosophical and political interpretation as that of pragmatic philosophies of Adam Smith...and Dewey, who define it as the right to exercise capitalist freedom even if it exceeds the needs of other classes of society....This is freedom at the expense of social and economic justice." On the other hand, Madani explained, "democracy in the Marxist sense...is a restriction of freedom....This system uses the rights of the group as an excuse." In contrast, he explained, "the Islamic alternative provides the kind of alternative where individual and societal freedoms do not oppose one another....In realizing justice and freedom without contradiction, Islamic shari'a...has gone beyond democracy and has achieved something not achieved in liberal or socialistic democracy." Thus, "we have only taken from democracy the return of expression of the people's right to choose their leadership. Other than that, our democracy is based on what Islam has brought in terms of total justice. Islam outlines a complete and just political system."

Madani's description of Islamic democracy as a distinct alternative to liberal and Marxist ideologies echoed the populist authoritarian ideology of the FLN. But we would be mistaken to see in FIS's ideology merely an Islamic version of Arab nationalism. After all, FIS claimed to speak for a revealed truth. Madani made this point at a fascinating moment in the interview, when he was asked whether an Islamic government would respect minority rights. Here is his response:

Islam is a religion which seeks the truth. One of its principles is *shura*, or mutual consultation, which encourages human... participation to achieve the truth. The truth, in this context cannot be measured exclusively by the minority or the majority. *The truth is the truth,* whether it is coming from the minority or the majority. If the majority is wrong and the minority...is right, then the right course of action lies with the minority. Islam requires its government to follow the truth, even if it is coming from a minority party. If the majority is right and the minority is wrong, then the two justifications are present: that of majority confirmation and of the truth. The truth must be followed. Thus, not only does the minority have the right to be present in the parliament, but also if it is right, the whole parliament must recognize that right, submit to it and adopt it. This means that we go beyond what is called "democracy" to what is higher and more complete.

In short, the purpose of politics was to realize the one transcendent "truth." That truth "must be followed" and "submitted to," whether it is expressed by a minority or majority. How his American audience responded to this a statement is anybody's guess. But one did not have to be familiar with the intricacies of utopian utilitarianism to sense that Madani's conception of "majority and minority" was absolutist to the core.

Madani's authoritarianism also surfaced in his discussion of the role of political parties. Madani insisted that Algeria's new parties "were founded for selfish, partisan reasons, and not for the people....These parties are lacking a historical base on which the will of the people is protected." Echoing the leaders of Egypt's Muslim Brethren, he added that "the difference between FIS and other parties is that the front does not want to be the ruling government party exclusively, but a party that offers guidance, historical usefulness....The other parties have been satisfied with copying social and political ideas...rather than studying and analyzing the true nature of society." In short, like his Egyptian analogues, Madani asserted that his party was above politics, a virtual beacon of light for the people. "The trust that the Algerian people have put in us," he insisted, was *not* in a reaction to the failure of the FLN and thus could

not be interpreted as a protest vote. Rather it was "an historical and political conviction...that the Algerian people are a Muslim people."

This said, Madani was not ready at this point to renounce the pragmatic gradualism that had gotten his party so far. Asked by the interviewer whether he believed that forces within the FLN were using the
prospect of a FIS regime "to scare Euro-oriented Algerians into supporting the FLN," he held out an olive branch to the FLN and by implication
to President Benjedid:

> The truth is that the FLN just like the FIS was noble in its princi-
> ples....It never compromised its principles until the end of the
> war....After the end of the revolution it became the ruling party and
> was infiltrated by opportunists...who deprived the party of its his-
> torical authenticity....If it [the FLN] regains its original spirit by re-
> turning to its principles, it will come back into the historical politi-
> cal process. We want the FLN to last, to be powerful so that it
> can...help us to make Algeria...strong. We want a strong front...not
> to be faced by the former corrupt, weak party. This opposition
> should strengthen the system of multi-party participation....The
> lion does not like to face himself...a lion needs someone to endan-
> ger him, to activate...his attention. We hope that the FLN will re-
> gain power and will stay a part of Algeria. There is nothing wrong
> with sharing power so long as power is for all the people.

At this point it was clear that Madani still believed that he could retain the support of President Chadli Benjedid by holding out the prospect that once the FLN had regained its "original spirit," the FIS could
envision sharing power with it. Perhaps in making this statement to an
American audience, he hoped that his seemingly conciliatory message
might be passed on to the Algerian president.[36]

But Madani miscalculated on two fronts. First, he could not hope to
gain the support of "regime soft-liners" and at the same time allow his
deputy, Ali Belhadj, to issue countless statements in which he unequivo-
cally promised to disenfranchise all secular Algerians. This approach alienated the FIS's potential allies in the middle class and discredited President Benjedid to the benefit of regime hard-liners—thus destroying the
basis for a democratic bargain.[37] Nor could Madani expect to strengthen

Benjedid's hand by insisting that the FLN would be welcomed back once it regained its "historical authenticity." FIS's utopian dream of "authenticity" was a nightmare for all Algerians who did not share it, or who did not embrace FIS's authoritarian rendering of it.

Conclusion

Why did the Algerian military wait as long as it did to put an end to this dream? Why did the regime not only fail to enforce its own constitution—which banned parties based strictly on religious or ethnicity—but also ignored the radical rhetoric of the FIS, which contradicted the spirit and letter of the constitution? The answer is that the splits within the regime opened the door for this escalation of events. From the outset, the military was opposed to Benjedid's reforms and only waited for the right moment to stop them. The FIS's leaders fell right into the trap.

I accentuate the role of Algeria's leaders because there is a tendency among students of Middle East politics to assign too much credit—or blame—to the part that Islamists play in advancing or undermining their own fortunes. Whatever the nature of Islamic ideology, it is states and their rulers that set and enforce the rules of the game. Rulers can live with reformist fundamentalism so long as they clearly and consistently lay down the boundaries beyond which Islamists will not be allowed to venture.

Comparative analysis suggests that some kinds of states are better suited to imposing such boundaries than others. Post-populist states such as Egypt and Algeria do an especially bad job, perhaps because their respective ruling parties and "revolutionary" leaders were expected to embody and enforce the "will" of a supposedly organic society. In contrast, some traditional monarchies such as Kuwait and Jordan appear better positioned to enforce limits, perhaps because they embody an autonomous state which mediates the disparate interests of acknowledged social mosaics. Still, it would be naïve to think that coexistence will alter the strategic vision of fundamentalist Islamists. Like their Jewish counterparts, they see the state merely as a vehicle for realizing (or obstructing) God's commandments.

What then of strategic modernism? Does it have a chance to take political root in the Middle East? For the moment it remains an intellectual force which depends on the state for protection. Islamic liberals have little base in society, and where they lack such as base or the state's protection, they often must flee to the West.[38] Only outside the Middle East, in Malaysia and Indonesia, has strategic modernism struck institutional roots in society. But in Southeast Asia, Islam grew out of a cultural, economic and institutional context that differed totally from that which shaped the modern Middle East. Some Arab Islamists are especially fascinated by Indonesia, where various Islamic movements thrive because an authoritarian, multi-ethnic state upholds a division between "church" and state that protects religious pluralism.[39] It may be an attractive model, but it is not yet available for export.

NOTES

1. See for example Yvonne Yazbeck Haddad, "Islamic Depictions of Christianity in the Twentieth Century: The Pluralism Debate and the Depiction of the Other,"*Journal of Islam and Muslim-Christian Relations* (forthcoming); idem, "Islamists and the Challenge of Pluralism," *Occasional Paper*, Center for Contemporary Arab Studies and Center for Muslim-Christian Understanding, Georgetown University, 1995; Salwa Ismail, "Democracy in Contemporary Arab Intellectual Discourse," in *Political Liberalization and Democratization in the Arab World*, eds. Rex Brynen et al. (Boulder: Reinner, 1995); Ahmad S. Moussalli, "Modern Fundamentalist Discourses on Civil Society, Pluralism and Democracy," in *Civil Society in the Middle East*, ed. August Richard Norton (2 vols.; London: Brill, 1995), 1:79-119.
2. Edward Mortimer, *Faith and Power: The Politics of Islam* (New York: Vintage Books, 1982), 16.
3. Ibid., 406.
4. Leonard Binder, *Islamic Liberalism: A Critique of Development Ideologies* (Chicago: University of Chicago Press, 1988), 95.
5. John Voll and John Esposito, "Islam's Democratic Essence," *Middle East Quarterly* 1, no. 3 (September 1994): 3-11.
6. Binder, *Islamic Liberalism*, 103.
7. Aziz Al-Azmeh, *Islams and Modernities* (London, Verso: 1993), 20 and 21-22 respectively.

8. All the following quotes are taken from Robin Wright's "Two Visions of Reformation" and the commentaries that follow it. See *Journal of Democracy* 7, no. 2 (April 1996): 64-89.
9. Voll and Esposito, "Islam's Democratic Essence."
10. Adam Przeworski, "Democracy as a Contingent Outcome of Conflicts," in *Constitutionalism and Democracy*, eds. Jon Elster and Rune Slagstad (Cambridge: Cambridge University Press, 1988), 58-80.
11. *Democracy Without Democrats? The Renewal of Politics in the Muslim World*, ed. Ghassan Salamé (London: Tauris, 1994).
12. Hasan al-Banna, "Between Yesterday and Today," in *Five Tracts of Hasan Al Banna*, trans. Charles Wendell (Los Angeles: University of California Press, 1978), 13-38.
13. The liberal Islamist Laith Kubba argues that under the influence of modern ideologies, contemporary Islamists have confused the notion of Islam's "comprehensiveness" with the idea of totalitarianism. He makes this point by using the word *shumuliyya* to mean both comprehensiveness and totalitarianism. See his "Shumuliyyat al-qim wa-khususiyyat al-mu'assasat," *Al-Mustaqilla*, 19 February 1996.
14. Al-Azmeh, *Islams*, 91.
15. Esposito and Voll, "Islam's Democratic Essence," 5, citing from Mawdudi's "Political Theory of Islam," in *Islam: Its Meanings and Message*, ed. Kurshid Ahmad (London: Islamic Council of Europe, 1976), 159-61.
16. Hasan Turabi, "The Islamic State," in *Voices of Resurgent Islam*, ed. John Esposito (Oxford: Oxford University Press, 1982), 241-51.
17. Ibid., 241.
18. Interview with Ma'mun al-Hudaybi, *Al-Mustaqilla*, 4 March 1996.
19. Al-Azmeh, *Islams*, 29.
20. *Civil Society* 5, no. 51 (March 1996): 25.
21. See Turabi, "The Islamic State." We shall see below that Abbasi Madani made a similar case in discussing the role of minorities and majorities.
22. See interview with Turabi, *Al-Mustaqilla*, 26 February 1996.
23. *Islam, Democracy, the State and the West: A Round Table with Dr. Hasan Turabi*, ed. Arthur L. Lowrie (Tampa, Florida: World and Islam Studies Enterprise, 1993), 56, 61. Emphasis mine. Turabi's authoritarian views had been clear since 1988 when, as minister of justice, he issued the notorious "September Laws." After the 1989 coup, he administered the repressive policies that earned Sudan one of the worst human rights records in the world. With few exceptions, the participants in the above discussion treated him with kid gloves.
24. Ibid., 98. Emphasis mine.
25. JPRS NEA-84-014. Unless otherwise indicated, this and the following Foreign Broadcast Information Service (FBIS) and Joint Publication Research Services (JPRS) citations are from Amy Jo Johnson, "Can Religious Groups Contribute to

Political Pluralism? An Analysis of the Role of the Muslim Brotherhood in Egyptian Parliamentary Elections" (bachelor's thesis, Department of Political Science, Emory University, 1992).

26. "Al-Talmasani Defines Muslim Brotherhood-Wafd Cooperation," JPRS NEA-84-177, 7 December 1984.

27. "Notion that Shariah Application Threatens Christians Refuted," JPRS NEA-84-109, 2 July 1984.

28. "Muslim Brotherhood Leader Interviewed," JPRS NEA-87-068, 23 June 1987.

29. Ibid.

30. "Moslem Brothers Instruct President on Foreign, Domestic Affairs," JPRS NEA-87-058, 22 May 22, 1987.

31. Ali Ben Hadj, "Seule la Charia" (interview), *Horizons*, 23 February 1989.

32. "FIS Chairman Holds New Conference," FBIS NES 90-008, 11 January 1990.

33. Interview with Madani in *Al-Watan*, 17 June 1990, in FBIS NES 90-124, 22 June 1990.

34. See Daniel Brumberg, "Islam, Elections, and Reform in Algeria," *Journal of Democracy* 2, no. 1 (Winter 1991): 58-71.

35. The tape, which was sent to the Carter Center of Emory University, was produced by "Pontifax," a Los Angeles company. The following quotes are taken from the tape.

36. The tape was sent to the Carter Center, and President Carter had maintained a special relationship with Algeria since the hostage crisis in 1979-80. In any case, all the evidence suggests that Madani was communicating his desire to work with Benjedid until the crisis of November 1990.

37. See Hugh Roberts, "From Radical Mission to Equivocal Ambition: The Expansion and Manipulation of Algerian Islamism, 1979-1992," in *Accounting for Fundamentalisms*, eds. Martin E Marty and R. Scott Appleby (Chicago: University of Chicago Press, 1994), 428-89. Roberts amply documents the hostile rhetoric employed by the FIS against the regime.

38. As the case of Dr. Nasr Abu Zayd sadly demonstrates. In the 27 January 1996 edition of *The Economist* appear two articles side by side. The first tells the story of Abu Zayd, the Egyptian modernist thinker forced to flee Egypt after a court declared his marriage null and void because he was an "apostate." On the right appears a review of Fred Halliday's *Islam and the Myth of Confrontation*. Apparently, the "Islamic threat" only concerns those in the West when it threatens them. Does this mean that if there is no threat to the West—as Halliday argues—we should ignore the threat that Islamic (and Jewish) fundamentalism poses to people in the Middle East like Abu Zayd?

39. See the very positive review of a book that examines Islam in Indonesia, *Al-Mustaqilla*, 12 February 1996.

Ballot Boxes, Militaries, and Islamic Movements

François Burgat

Ezra Pound once pointed out that it is the habit of democracy to tell two lies (one Labor, one Tory or one Democrat, one Republican) and then sit back to argue which one is actually true....The Ezra Pound effect has meant quarreling over whether the so-called Islamic fundamentalists are outright terrorists or just plain anti-secular fanatics. In this bipolar debate, the third alternative—that theirs is a political campaign that uses the religious discourse to promote radical social change and oppose government dishonesty and corruption—has become severely silenced.[1]

The more I am asked to comment on politics in general and violence in particular in the Arab world, the more I feel I should refrain from invoking the words "Islam," "fundamentalism," and "Islamic movements"— and the more I conclude that dominant representation of political violence in the Middle East tends to be "over-ideologized."

The two terrains of political violence in the Middle East are international and internal. The first one is not on my agenda here, especially as I have been asked to focus upon the situation in the Arab world: it is the Palestinian-Israeli conflict, an international conflict in which antagonistic representations of local history have produced a well-known process of growing bilateral confrontation and violence. It would require more time that I intend to use to document the idea that the level of Palestinian antagonism toward Israel is not strictly related to the terminology (secular or "religious") of the political actors but to the level of violence to which Palestinians are themselves exposed. The conclusions I have long advocated are that the willingness of an internal or international political actor to turn to violence (that of the "secularist" Saddam Husayn no

François Burgat is a research fellow at the Institut de Recherches et d'Etudes sur le Monde Arabe et Musulman, Aix-en-Provence.

less than that of "fundamentalist" Khomeini) is most directly related to both their educational and social background and, above all, to the norms of their own political environment. This is much more important than the brand of terminology which they use to mobilize their militants or express their demands.[2] Opposition to the terms, or to the obvious limits, of the Oslo-Cairo agreements have in fact arisen just as much from the secularist left of the Palestinian political landscape (DFLP and PFLP, headed moreover by Christian-born leaders) as from the "Islamic" movement. And if the "Islamic" resistance seems to have taken over the "secularist" generation, one must keep in mind that this reflects a process underway in all Arab settings.

The second main terrain of political violence which I intend to investigate very briefly is related to the internal situation of each of the Middle Eastern societies, and a direct outcome of each of its political systems. I do not have the proper knowledge to compare "Arab" political violence with the specific forms of tension which have developed inside Israeli society, such as that which has led to the assassination of the late prime minister, Yitzhak Rabin. I still think that a comparison ought to stress the idea that extremist political violence has developed in Israel in a context of political liberalism and democracy which presently has no equivalent on the Arab side.

Dominant representations of the Arab political scene in the 1980s and 1990s often depict a few secularist democrats struggling from inside fragile "civil societies" against battalions of "fundamentalists" who reject democracy and modernity just as much as they hate "peace," women or human rights. I would rather advance the idea that the line of fracture which splits almost all southern Mediterranean society nowadays does not segregate between an "anti-foreigner, anti-Christian, anti-Jewish, anti-women, anti-moderate, anti-government and anti-technology" group of fundamentalists on one side, and "the rest of the society," the "normal people," on the other. My understanding is that the fracture involved is triple: political, socio-economic, and cultural.

A Political Cleavage

The political fracture is the result of the refusal of the generation in power to admit any form of institutional regulation which may provoke its loss of political hegemony. It is a very "ordinary" conflict between a generation which has been in power for the last thirty years and a new political generation which feels entitled to gain access to the political system and is not permitted to do so. The common denominator of contemporary Arab regimes is their ability to promote "cosmetic" democratization, "for the Yankees to see,"[3] and to deny the real political forces access to the parliamentary game. In the name of "protecting democracy" and "elections," considered pluralist by most Western political observers, access to parliament is denied to the most representative political forces. In Egypt, as in Tunisia, Algiers and Morocco, not to mention Libya, the most important political forces (i.e., the Islamic parties) are prohibited from gaining legal recognition. Since casting votes has little or no effect on the balance of political forces, a shift of legitimacy inevitably occurs and enhances the efficiency of stone- or bomb-throwers. In Algeria, the December 1991 parliamentary elections, which had resulted in an unexpected majority for the Islamic party, were canceled. The presidential elections of November 1995 (which President Jacques Chirac of France, among other Western leaders, praised as "satisfyingly democratic") excluded the previous winners of both local and parliamentary elections from participation.

In Tunisia, whose "experience of modernization" has been labeled "exemplary" by Chirac, the ruling party has been returned by 99 percent of the votes. The most recent parliamentary elections in Egypt, in November 1995, have given a renewed example of both the technique by which a military regime can organize absolutely fraudulent elections and the recurrent willingness of most Western media to laud them for doing it. In 1990, the president of the French senate came to Cairo during elections which were being boycotted by all major opposition forces. The purpose of the visit was to present President Mubarak with a "democracy and human rights" honor prize. The ceremony was shown several times on national television between the two election days. In the same Egypt, elections of the leaders of unions, university faculties and municipalities have been cancelled, for fear of Islamist successes. Deans of faculties and mayors of municipalities are no longer elected. In the name of "promoting democracy," a law has put most unions under judicial control. From Cairo to Algiers, the lack of institutional regulation requires a growing level of repression. The use of torture against almost every individual facing a "political" accusation has become a customary means of political regulation, for 34,000 prisoners in Algeria (late 1995) and probably a lot more in Egypt.

It is this vicious combination of repression and lack of institutional regulation which is the main explanation for 90 percent of political violence in the contemporary Arab world. To a certain extent, we might describe the situation by saying that Arab regimes have the opponents they deserve. Arab regimes are the tutors of their opponents. They are responsible for most of their opponents' political behavior just as we Westerners have the international opposition we deserve. Over-ideologizing our reading of this political conflict may well be the easy way to refuse to face our share of responsibility in it. All of us carry our share of political responsibility for some of the "Islamic violence."

But featuring the political dimension of the violence does not mean that the socio-economic background ought to be ignored or even minimized.

A Socio-Economic Fracture

The second "line of fracture" may indeed be represented as an economic one between the "haves" and the "have nots." There is no doubt that political opponents are more likely to appear among those social groups which have been kept on the "wrong side" of development, housing, education and employment policies. Deteriorating economic conditions do produce political opposition. More social or economic disarray does radicalize political opponents and feed the process of violence.

But the economic factor does not determine the brand of vocabulary—secularist or "religious"—that political actors will eventually choose in order to express their demands. The dominant economic understanding tends to consider the Islamic movement as a mere pathology which can be dealt with through economic development. But this can be refuted by at least two types of counter-examples. Most wealthy oil economies such as Saudi Arabia and Kuwait have produced a strong brand of Islamic militancy, whether in power or in opposition. And to borrow from contemporary French history, France's failure to master the Algerian national movement in the late 1950s by implementing the Marshall-type "Plan de Constantine" equally demonstrates the limits of over-estimating the economic dimension of a political and "identitarian" mobilization. All the IMF's reserves would probably lower the level of political tensions in the Arab world, but it would not make nationalist or "democratic" demands vanish, nor would it affect the choice by a majority of people to use an "Islamic" vocabulary to express them.

A Cultural Fracture

For the third component of the process producing political violence in most Arab society nowadays, we must recall the cultural cleavage directly inherited from the nineteenth-century process of colonization.

In Algeria (which probably represents the archetype of the colonial relation to the West) and also in most of the other ex-colonial south Mediterranean societies, one component of the social fabric has interiorized the references of modernization using the terminology of Western culture, while other components of the same society are more acquainted with the universe of Muslim culture. As an aspect of decolonization, the "system of representation" (cultural codes, political discourse, social norms) tends to reconnect with the categories, terminology, and vocabulary of Muslim culture, after a period of time when these categories had been marginalized, discredited, or simply "folklorized" by the brief hegemony of Western culture. Sharp delineations are inadequate to describe a complex reality of multiple and changing allegiances. One rather ought to say that most contemporary Arab individuals mobilize a double system of symbolic allegiances.

Such a dual symbolic system can be a source of strength and special talents. Many citizens of Israel, for example, most probably have experienced this advantage of having a dual linguistic system, a dual cultural belonging, and they are able to function confidently in a double symbolic universe.

However, if the communication between the two systems is not absolutely unimpeded and independent, if there are unilateral interferences by the educational or even more by the political system, preventing the use of one system or imposing it, the dualism may no longer be a source of strength but of schizophrenia. It may generate conflicts and reactionary, radical, self-defensive attitudes. When this type of conflict combines with a political mobilization, and especially if this political mobilization happens to be part of a civil war, this complex "cultural" fracture may produce very sharp dividing lines, tearing apart a unique social or even family environment. The fracture which isolates a member of the Islamic Salvation Front from a member of the National Liberation Front can very well tear apart the same middle class family, leaving one son supporting the "Islamic" camp and another fighting against it. This third line of fracture segregates between those who have interiorized modernization using the terminology of Western culture, and those who prefer expressing their demands, be they social or political, using the terminology of Muslim culture and promoting the broad process of "re-Islamization" of the system of representation.

The re-Islamization process has long been exploited in politics both by the regimes and their opponents. Both have tried to instrumentalize this demand to reconnect the process of producing modernity with the use of the categories of the popular local culture. But the role of an elite in promoting secularist reforms (often implemented, as in Atatürk's Turkey, against the institutions of traditional Islamic culture), tends to lower the credibility of "state fundamentalism," such as that promoted by Egyptian populist television preachers who support the regime against "fundamentalism against the state."

For Westerners, especially in the former colonial powers, the process of re-Islamization is difficult to deal with rationally: it tends to dispute our ideological hegemony and the feeling we have had of some kind of monopoly of expressing modernity. It feeds many irrational and emotional assessments which leave little space for the studies and analysis urgently required by the rise of bilateral tensions.

On the contrary, Algeria's civil war tends to become the main reservoir of material used to represent the entire dynamic of opposition to all Arab military regimes. Attitudes and discourses of the radicalized armed Islamic groups (or of the secret service which manipulates many of them) are invariably invoked to produce a one-sided, monolithic and repellent image of all forces linked to the Islamic opposition. This serves to legitimize both the repressive policy of the militaries in power, and the discourse of that component of the Arab secularist elite which has chosen to support them.

Islam and Modernization

Along with the radical discourse of the "exclusivist" Arab secularist elite, most Western intellectuals tend to perceive the process of re-Islamization as a mere process of re-traditionalization, developing in a relation of antinomy and exclusion to the dynamic of political liberalization and social modernization. Since the nineteenth century, and due to the colonial presence, Arab elites also have identified the one-time process of social and political "modernization" as a mere process of "Westernization."

But the endogenous "Islamic" reaction can be considered an attempt to reconnect the process of modernization with the terminology of the local endogenous culture, an attempt by Muslims to gain the right to express modernization, progress, science, and universal values, no longer by reference to the categories of a Western civilization once identified with colonialism and military occupation.

Can Islamic terminology accommodate the "de-traditionalization" of women's status, can it help the slow and difficult process which will guarantee their autonomy inside the family space and their access to education, the professions, and politics? Can it accommodate pluralism, some kind of autonomy of politics from religion and, last but not least, can it accommodate democracy?

To both of the two questions of whether the "Islamic movement" clearly contradicts or endangers the process of social modernization and political liberalization, the hard core of my previous approach can be summarized by a prudent but clearly negative answer. It would be very difficult to document the idea that the impact of re-Islamization can be described in terms of "re-traditionalization" or "de-modernization." Although I do not intend to document this hypothesis, I shall mention that my own conclusion converges with that of an increasing number of similar studies.

I do not think that a rational long-term understanding of Arab political dynamics can demonize the political forces linked to the Islamic movement. Today, in politics, Islam's vocabulary is very likely to remain part of our short-term future universe. It ought not to be considered, in itself, the main source of our present difficulty in facing this future.

NOTES

1. James Toth, "Islamic Activism as an Avenue of Radical Social Change" (paper presented at the International Association of Middle Eastern Studies, Sixth Congress, University of Al Al-Bayt, Mafraq, Jordan, 10-14 April 1996).
2. I have developed my general understanding of the Islamic movement in these works: *L'Islamisme au Maghreb: la voix du Sud* (Paris: Karthala, 1988 and Payot, 1995); *The Islamic Movement in North Africa* (Austin, Texas: University of Texas Press, 1993); and *L'Islamisme en face* (Paris: La Decouverte, 1996).
3. Nazih Ayubi, *Over-Stating the Arab State* (London: Tauris, 1995), 411.

DISCUSSION

Judith Miller *(New York Times):* I agree that modernization is something the West cannot monopolize, since Asia presents an alternative model of modernization, different from that of Western democracies. But where do you see an Islamic modernization taking place? Especially when the one thing we do know about modernization is that it requires some minimal level of participation and education? In the Islamic systems, there are many areas in which women cannot participate. There are many areas in which minorities, or minority groups, are not full citizens. How can this possibly facilitate modernization?

François Burgat: Regarding women, it is difficult for me to speak about Iran in the presence of specialists on this subject. But I rely upon most studies of the social participation of women inside Iranian society, and if I am not mistaken, the rate of women's employment in public administration in Iran is the highest in the region. Women social scientists who have described the social dynamics inside an Islamic environment always give the same answer: the participation of women is not easy, it takes time, but it moves forward. If we admit that guaranteeing access to education and employment can be called universal modernization, most observers of Iran admit that the status of the women—not of a tiny fringe of Westernized women, but women in the entire society—has advanced during the last fifteen years.

At the more theoretical level, I would say that when I refer to the Islamic movement as a medium of modernization, I refer to its ability to restore the legitimacy of the state's connections with the individual. Let me give an example. A very interesting survey was done four years ago in Egypt, saying that over 92 percent of the people would not put one single Egyptian pound in the bank. Now suddenly the option of Islamic banks is offered (I am leaving aside just what an "Islamic bank" is), and lo and behold, people from Upper Egypt take the money out from under their mattresses for the first time in their lives and put it in wider circulation. In every language on earth, this deserves to be called modernization. It connects people. There are those who ask, what can Islamists do in the field of economy? I say they can tap the one tank which is not empty, social mobilization. I am not saying that this is a magic formula, but sometimes it works. Islamists can restore the ability of the state to communicate with the individual. This ability had been destroyed by the Nasserist type of modernization, because it tried to eradicate any infrastate structure which was perceived as antagonistic to the hegemony of the state.

When you go to Cairo, the main avenues are clean and the narrow streets are dirty. The state is efficient in the main avenues of power. But in the alleys, not only is it unable to be efficient, but it prevents anyone else from being efficient in its place. This is the vicious side of the Nasserist type of modernization. I myself interviewed people, asking them: you are supposedly an Islamist, previously you were a Nasserist. Why did you shift? As one of my interviewees put it: "I have understood that there is no way for the state to communicate efficiently with society, without the medium of religious culture."

Participant: Islamist violence looks more like a preference than a reaction. In Jordan, the state closely restricts the options of the Islamists, and so the Islamists are moderate in Jordan. Constrained by the state, the Islamists do what they can. If they are more radical in a place like Algeria, it is because there are fewer constraints, the state is weaker, the preference for violence can play itself out.

François Burgat: We have to go into the question of who is responsible for the violence in Algeria. The regime in Algeria does not fear those who throw bombs, it fears those who cast ballots. They are the enemy. The successful FIS electoral campaign in 1990 required no intellectuals to be slaughtered, no women to be raped. And the violence that came later cannot be regarded as the perfect example of the preference of the Islamists when there are no limits. When the process of elections was interrupted in December 1991, Abd al-Qadir Hashani was the head of the FIS. He was the most moderate person you could imagine, and he was receiving phone calls from major Islamic leaders—from Jordanians and Palestinians, from London—telling him: slow down. Don't take power, keep cool, be patient, don't reply with weapons. Those who wanted violence were the tiny hard core of the military, who knew that they had completely lost their political legitimacy.

When we see different brands of militants, the variable is the violence employed against them. Inside Palestine, for example, you have two brands of political Islamists. One of them emerged in a Jordanian environment, in the West Bank; the other, in an Egyptian environment, in Gaza. If you were an Islamist in an Egyptian environment, you lived in the atmosphere of the repression of the Muslim Brethren. The entire political culture of the Egyptian Muslim Brethren is torture, repression and jail. But if you were an Islamic militant in a Jordanian environment, you had a more sophisticated relationship with the regime. This explains the differences. As I said, you get the political opponents you deserve. There are exceptions—there are fringe extremists in every society—but not 50 or 60 percent or more of a people.

Islam is only a reference. If a young fellow living in the suburbs of Algiers has been expelled from the economic system and left jobless, then expelled by force, violence and torture from the political system because he has had the insolence to win an election, then this fellow will pick up the tiny fringe of the religious reference which allows him, entitles him, to use any kind of violence. In contrast, in a place like Jordan, as it was for example in 1990, the most extreme product will be a Layth Shubaylat, who is more moderate by miles than an Ali Belhadj or an Abbud al-Zumur. To understand the inner dynamics of Islamist movements, you must thoroughly know which environment activists have experienced on their road to activism.

Give me any political party in the West, and I will transform it into the Armed Islamic Group within weeks, if I employ the same methods which have been used against the Islamic movement, with our funding, over the last five years.

Daniel Brumberg: I tend to agree with you: if those who take a gradualist position can be integrated into the system without threatening it, that certainly is a better option than repression. As you say, repression has outcomes which can be dangerous. But what would have been the best approach for the regime in Algeria? One solution might have been simply to insist that the FIS sign a national charter of some kind, declaring the rules of the game. Another solution might simply have been to put aside the issue of elections and first promote a gradual political liberalization. What would have been the best approach in your view?

François Burgat: Remember that it was not Chadli who stopped the elections. He had used them as a lever against rivals in the FLN, and he was willing to go through and toy with the experiment. When the elections were aborted, Chadli was president. Look at the Algerian constitution. When you are president, you are God; the parliament is nothing. The army was at his command, and at any time could have done what it did do two weeks later. My answer is easy: they should have let the parliamentarians chosen by the people assume their responsibilities, knowing that the parliament could not amend the constitution, that the president could lock the entire system, and that the army could intervene at any time were it necessary.

Ibrahim Karawan (International Institute of Strategic Studies, London): I cannot see eye to eye with you about this supposed link between state repression over a period of time and the methods of the militants. You submit that the state produced the kind of opposition it now faces, and that a different outcome would have been possible had there been more participation and democracy. Perhaps this is partly true regarding some of those who may be called political Islamists, and who could conceivably be integrated into the system. But in the case of Egypt, I wish you could help me understand the link between the escalation of violence in Egypt against Copts and tourists, and whatever restriction the state did or did not place on the scope of political participation. The writers and theoreticians of the Islamist militant movements say that their main motive for action was that they felt that their cause was being compromised by the Muslim Brethren for agreeing to operate within the boundaries of the system, legitimizing what should not be legitimized, which is the rule of humans over the rule of *shari'a*. I too am in favor of expanding the scope of participation. But I fail to see the link between acts of violence against Copts or tourists, and the level of political participation.

François Burgat: You postulate that Islam is the rule of God and democracy is the rule of humans. There are Islamists who would reply that there is space for profane law inside an Islamic system. If the Muslims must decide tomorrow whether to drive on the right side or the left side of the road, there is no guidance in the Sunna or in Islamic jurisprudence.

But is our own democracy really absolute majority rule, the sovereignty only of the people? Assume we sit in a parliament that decides that the majority shall slaughter the minority. How many seconds will it take for the minority to remind us that this violates a higher principle? Even within liberal political thought, there are principles which are out of range of human will. In the United States and in many European countries, these are grounded in the religious teachings of the Bible. In France we would call them *droit naturel* or *principes généraux du droit*. We have never abandoned the idea that human will has its limits.

But if we are speaking of majority rule, I would say this: let the majority express itself in this part of the world and I think that most of the political contradictions will dissolve. There is not one single country where the population is entitled to choose. Let the majority express itself politically, and then we shall all support the result of the poll.

You ask for an explanation for the violence against tourists and the Copts. First, we should not take violence against the Copts as the main gate through which to enter into a political understanding of the situation in Egypt.

Ibrahim Karawan: Why not?

François Burgat: Because although it exists (on a limited scale), it is also a major instrument of communication by the regime with the West. The responsibility of the regime is probably more than it seems. In many circumstances, when these events occur, the scenario is similar. There is extremism in the local Islamic groups, there can be no doubt about it. But the regime also benefits immensely whenever these things happen, and this too is undeniable. When trouble starts, the police do nothing, and the trouble spreads. And then the police come and arrest seven or eight hundred of the Islamic militants, and no one on the other side. This then feeds the idea among Muslims that the Copts do not share the same struggle. Islamic militants then feel that the Copts are being instrumentalized by the regime against them. This analysis is not an excuse. It is an explanation of why this violence is not part of the structural violence of the system.

A television program came to me in Cairo and wanted me to speak about the relationship of the Islamic movement to the Copts. I said: If you want to hear about the riots, anyone can explain them to you. Let me give you another sort of information. Here is an Islamic newspaper, *Al-Sha'b*. Look at page three. See the photograph of the man with a great black beard. He is not an Islamist, he is a priest, and he has a quarter of a page each week inside an Islamic newspaper to explain his point of view. So this is also a reality of the political scene in Egypt: the Islamic opposition does have links and connections with Christians, and they cooperate. But this doesn't make the news and prime time. What does make the headlines is what I would call ethnic or traditional riots in Upper Egypt. I condemn them, but they are not the main entrance into an understanding of the political dynamics in the country.

When it comes to the tourists, you cannot understand these attacks unless you enter into your analysis the violence which was showered on the Islamic movement between 1990 and 1992. It produced a decision to hit the regime by striking at the economy of tourism. Of course it is condemnable, but it is a rational internal strategy. Tourism fuels the state; I hate whatever fuels the state; this is a civil war; therefore I strike tourists. But this is not part of an ideological revulsion against foreign tourists.

Participant: How do you explain the repressive policies in the south of the Sudan? You cannot say that this is a reaction to state repression of the Muslims.

François Burgat: I am not supporting the regime of Sudan, but let me say this. In 1992, I heard the United Nations Program Development officer responsible for Sudan label the achievements of the Sudanese in the field of agriculture a "very badly advertised little miracle." This regime has done things; you cannot just throw away the entire political experience in Sudan.

It is true that they are repressive. But to what extent? We must criticize Sudan, but if we want to be efficient in our criticism, we must use the same standards we refuse to apply when it comes to Saudi Arabia, Egypt, Syria, Algeria, and Tunisia. I second the criticism of Sudan, it is a regime I do not support. But I would also assert that the level of political violence which the Sudanese regime uses nowadays to stay in power is much lower than the level of violence required by the Egyptian, Algerian, and Saudi regimes.

Are Islamists Ideological or Pragmatic?

Ideological, argues Daniel Pipes—and their ideology has its roots in the Western tradition of radicalism. Pragmatic, replies Olivier Roy: wherever Islamists hold power, expediency defines the role of Islam.

The Western Mind of Radical Islam

Daniel Pipes

Fathi al-Shiqaqi, a well-educated young Palestinian living in Damascus, recently boasted of his familiarity with European literature. He told an interviewer how he had read and enjoyed Shakespeare, Dostoyevsky, Chekhov, Sartre, and T.S. Eliot. He spoke of his particular passion for Sophocles' *Oedipus Rex*, a work he read ten times in English translation "and each time wept bitterly."[1] Such acquaintance with world literature and such exquisite sensibility would not be of note except for two points—that Shiqaqi was, until his assassination in Malta in late 1995, a fundamentalist Muslim and that he headed Islamic Jihad, the arch-terrorist organization that has murdered dozens of Israelis over the last two years.

Shiqaqi's familiarity with things Western fits a common pattern. His successor as head of Islamic Jihad was Ramadan Abdullah Shallah, a scholar who had previously lived in Britain and the United States for nine years and who, at the time of Shiqaqi's death, taught political science at the University of South Florida in Tampa. Iyad Isma'il, one of the World Trade Center bombers recently extradited from Jordan, also had a special affection for the United States. According to his brother, "He loved everything American from cowboy movies to hamburgers."[2] His sister recalled his love of American television and his saying "I want to live in America forever." The family, she commented, "always considered him a son of America."[3]

Islamist intellectuals are also very much at home in the West. Hasan al-Turabi, the effective ruler of Sudan, the man behind the notorious "ghost houses" and the brutal persecution of his country's large Christian minority, often flaunts his knowledge of the West, telling a French interviewer that most fundamentalist leaders, like himself, are "from the Christian, Western culture. We speak your languages."[4] In a statement that sums up this whole outlook, a fundamentalist in Washington asserted, "I listen to Mozart; I read Shakespeare; I watch the Comedy Channel; and I also believe in the implementation of the *shari'a* [Islamic sacred law]."[5]

Daniel Pipes is the editor of the Philadelphia-based *Middle East Quarterly*.

This pattern points to a paradox: the very intellectuals intent on marching the Muslim world back to the seventh century also excel in Western ways and seem very much to appreciate at least some of them. How does this happen? What does it indicate about their present strengths and future course?

Fundamentalists are Westernized

Fundamentalist leaders tend to be well acquainted with the West, having lived there, learned its languages, and studied its cultures. Turabi of the Sudan has advanced degrees from the University of London and the Sorbonne; he also spent a summer in the United States, touring the country on a U.S. taxpayer-financed program for foreign student leaders. Abbasi Madani, a leader of Algeria's Islamic Salvation Front (FIS), received a doctorate in education from the University of London. His Tunisian counterpart, Rashid al-Ghannushi, spent a year in France, and since 1993 makes his home in Great Britain. Necmettin Erbakan, Turkey's leading militant politician and now its prime minister, studied in Germany. Musa Muhammad Abu Marzuq, the head of Hamas's political committee, has lived in the U.S. since 1980, has a doctorate degree in engineering from the University of Louisiana, and has been a permanent U.S. resident since 1990. In recent years he lived in northern Virginia with his wife and six children.[6] He was arrested in 1995 at a New York airport on his way into the country to register his son in an American school.

Indeed, the experience of living in the West often turns indifferent Muslims into fundamentalists. Discussing Mehdi Bazargan, an Iranian engineer who spent the years 1928-35 in France, Hamid Dabashi dissects the process many Muslim students undergo.

> Beginning with the conscious or unconscious, articulated or mute, premise that they ought to remain firmly attached to their Islamic consciousness, they begin to admire "The Western" achievements....They recognize a heightened state of ideological self-awareness on the part of "The West" that they identify as the source and cause of its achievements. They then look back at their own society where such technological achievements were lacking, a fact

they attribute, in turn, to the absence of that heightened state of ideological self-awareness.[7]

The key notion here, the French analyst Olivier Roy explains, is the rather surprising notion that ideologies are "the key to the West's technical development." This assumption leads fundamentalists "to develop a modern political ideology based on Islam, which they see as the only way to come to terms with the modern world and the best means of confronting foreign imperialism."[8] Some of the leading fundamentalists fit this pattern. The Egyptian Sayyid Qutb went to the United States in 1948 as an admirer of things American, then "returned" to Islam during his two years of residence there, becoming one of the most influential fundamentalist thinkers of our time. Ali Shari'ati of Iran lived five years in Paris, 1960-65; from this experience came the key ideas of the Islamic revolution. In other cases, fundamentalist thinkers do not actually live in the West but absorb its ways at a distance by learning a Western language and immersing themselves in Western ideas, as did the Indo-Pakistani journalist, thinker and politician Sayyid Abul A'la Mawdudi (1903-79). In still other cases, reading Western works in translation serves just as well. Morteza Motahhari, a leading acolyte of Khomeini's, made as thorough a study of Marxism as possible in the Persian language.

Many of fundamentalism's intellectual lights share a background of technical accomplishment. Erbakan quickly rose to the top of the engineering profession in Turkey as a full professor at Istanbul Technical University, director at a factory producing diesel motors, and even head of the country's Chamber of Commerce. Layth Shubaylat, a Jordanian firebrand, is also president of the Jordanian Engineers Association. These men take special pride in being able to challenge the West in the area of its greatest strength.

Actual terrorists also tend to be science-oriented, though less accomplished. Ramzi Yusuf, the accused mastermind of the World Trade Center bombing, is an electronics engineer and explosives expert, with an advanced degree from the Swansea Institute in South Wales, Britain;[9] Nidal Ayyad was an up-and-coming chemical engineer at Allied Signal; and Iyad Isma'il studied computers and engineering at Wichita State University.[10] This same pattern holds in the Middle East: Salah Ali Uthman, one of three terrorists who attacked a bus in Jerusalem on 1 July 1993, was a student of computer science at the University in Gaza.[11] The most notorious anti-Zionist terrorist of recent years is one Yahya Ayyash, nicknamed "The Engineer."

Fundamentalist knowledge of the West seems to focus on engineering and comedies, but it is not limited to that. In a statement of beliefs from his Manhattan jail cell, Ramzi Yusuf cited the *Encyclopedia Britannica* and *The New York Times*, as well as one of Newton's laws of physics.[12] This man is no bumpkin. One of his friends says that the remarkable thing about Ramzi Yusuf was his apparent pleasure in learning about new languages, cultures, and peoples, then proceeding to blow them up.[13] So much knowledge of the West demonstrates that fundamentalists are not peasants living in the unchanging countryside but modern, thoroughly urbanized individuals, many of them university graduates.

Notwithstanding all their talk about recreating the society of the Prophet Muhammad, fundamentalists are modern individuals at the forefront of coping with modern life. These are women struggling to keep their virtue on extremely packed buses, entrepreneurs attempting to live by the Qur'anic strictures on usury, and engineers working out the spiritual significance of the computer.

Ignorance of Traditional Islam

In contrast to this ostentatious familiarity with Western ways, fundamentalists are distant from their own culture. Turabi admitted to a French interviewer, "I know the history of France better than the history of Sudan, I love your culture, your painters, your musicians."[14] He offered no comparable praise for Sudanese painters and musicians. Having found Islam on their own as adults, many fundamentalists are ignorant of their own history and traditions. Some of "the new generation of Islamic fundamentalists," Martin Kramer notes, "are born-again Muslims, ill-acquainted with Islamic tradition."[15] Tunisia's minister of religion, Ali Chebbi, goes further, saying that "they ignore the fundamental facts of Islam."[16] Like Mawdudi, these autodidacts mix a bit of this and that, as Seyyed Vali Reza Nasr explains:

Mawdudi's formulation was by no means rooted in traditional Islam. He adopted modern ideas and values, mechanisms, procedures, and idioms, weaving them into an Islamic fabric....he sought not to resurrect an atavistic order but to modernize the traditional conception of Islamic thought and life. His vision represented a clear break with Islamic tradition and a fundamentally new reading of Islam which took its cue from modern thought.[17]

On reflection, this lack of knowledge should not be surprising. Fundamentalists are individuals educated in modern ways who seek solutions to modern problems; of course they know the West's ways better than their own country's traditions. The Prophet may inspire, but they approach him through the filter of the late twentieth century. In the process, they unintentionally substitute Western ways for those of traditional Islam.

Traditional Islam—the immensely rewarding faith of nearly a billion adherents—developed a civilization that for over a millennium gave order to the lives of young and old, rich and poor, sophisticate and ignorant, Moroccan and Malaysian. Alienated from this tradition, fundamentalists dispense with it in the chimerical effort to return to the pure and simple ways of Muhammad. To connect spiritually to the first years of Islam, when the Prophet was alive and the faith was new, they seek to skip back thirteen centuries. The most mundane issues inspire them to recall the Prophet's times. Thus, an author portrays the "survival tactics" employed by Muslim students at American universities to retain their Islamic identity as "much like the early Muslims during the Hijra [from Mecca to Medina]."[18]

Fundamentalists see themselves not as tradition-bound but as engaged in a highly novel enterprise. According to Iran's spiritual leader, Ali Khamenei, "The Islamic system that the imam [Khomeini] created...has not existed in the course of history, except at the beginning [of Islam]."[19] Ghannushi similarly asserts that "Islam is ancient but the Islamist movement is recent."[20] In rejecting a whole millennium, the fundamentalists throw out a great deal of their own legacy, from the great corpus of Qur'anic scholarship to the finely worked interpretations of law. They are not absorbed by the splendors of mosque architecture.

On the contrary, they admire efficient factories and armies. For them, no less than for a Swedish aid official, the Muslim world is backward, and they too urgently seek its overhaul through the application of modern means. When this process goes slowly, they blame the West for withholding its technology. Thus, Ali Akbar Mohtashemi, the Iranian archradical, plaintively bemoans that "the United States and the West will never give us the technology" to pursue what he quaintly calls "the science of industrialization."[21] The fundamentalists' goal turns out to be not a genuinely Islamic order but an Islamic-flavored version of Western reality. This is particularly apparent in four areas: religion, daily life, politics, and the law.

Imitating Christianity

It is certainly not their intent, but fundamentalist Muslims have introduced some distinctly Christian notions into their Islam.

Church-like structure. Traditional Islam was characterized by informal organizations. Virtually every major decision—establishing a canonical text of the Qur'an, excluding philosophical inquiry, or choosing which religious scholars to heed—was reached in an unstructured and consensual way. This has been the genius of the religion, and it meant that rulers who tried to control the religious institution usually failed. Fundamentalists, ignorant of this legacy, have set up church-like structures. The trend began in Saudi Arabia, where the authorities built a raft of new institutions. Already in 1979, Khalid Durán wrote about the emergence of a "priestly hierarchy with all its churchly paraphernalia":

> A number of religious functionaries have come into being whose posts were previously unheard of, for example: the Secretary of the Muslim World League, the Secretary General of the Islamic Conference, the Rector of the Islamic University in Medina, and so [on] and so forth. For the first time in history the imam of the Ka'ba has been sent on tour of foreign countries as if he were an Apostolic Nuntius.[22]

The Islamic Republic of Iran soon followed the Saudi model and went beyond it, Shahrough Akhavi explains, to institute a Catholic-style control of the clergy:

> The centralization that has occurred in the religious institution in Iran is unprecedented, and actions have been taken that resemble patterns in the ecclesiastical church tradition familiar in the West. For example, in 1982, Khomeini encouraged the "defrocking" and "excommunication" of his chief rival, Ayatollah Muhammad Kazim Shari'atmadari (d. 1986), although no machinery for this has ever existed in Islam. Other trends, such as centralized control over budgets, appointments to the professorate, curricula in the seminaries, the creation of religious militias, monopolizing the representation of interests, and mounting a Kulturkampf in the realm of the arts, the family, and other social issues tell of the growing tendency to create an "Islamic episcopacy" in Iran.

Even more striking, Akhavi notes, is how Khomeini made himself pope:

> Khomeini's practice of issuing authoritative fatwas, obedience to which is made compulsory, comes close to endowing the top jurist with powers not dissimilar to those of the pope in the Catholic Church. After all, compliance with a particular cleric's fatwas in the past had not been mandatory.[23]

In creating this faux Christian hierarchy, fundamentalists invented something more Western than Islamic.

Friday as sabbath. In a similar confusion, fundamentalists have turned Fridays into a sabbath, something it had not previously been. Traditionally, Friday was a day of congregating for prayer, not a day of rest. Indeed, the whole idea of sabbath is alien to the vehemently monotheistic spirit of Islam, which deems the notion of God needing a day of rest falsely anthropomorphic. Instead, the Qur'an (62:9-10) instructs Muslims to "leave off business" only while praying; once finished, they should "disperse through the land and seek God's bounty"—in other words, engage in commerce. A day of rest so smacks of Jewish and Christian practice, some traditional Islamic authorities actually discouraged taking Friday off. In most places and times, Muslims did work on Fridays, interrupted only by the communal service.

In modern times, Muslim states imitated Europe and adopted a day of rest. The Ottoman Empire began closing government offices on Thursday, a religiously neutral day, in 1829. Christian imperialists imposed Sunday as the weekly day of rest throughout their colonies, a practice Muslim rulers adopted as well; for example, the Republic of Turkey did so in 1935. Upon independence, virtually every Muslim government inherited the Sunday rest and maintained it. S. D. Goitein, the foremost scholar of this subject, notes that Muslim states did so "in response to the exigencies of modern life and in imitation of Western precedent."[24] Recently, as the Sunday sabbath came to be seen as too Western, Muslim rulers asserted their Islamic identities by instituting Friday as the day off. Little did they realize that, in so doing, they perpetuated a specifically Judeo-Christian custom. And as Fridays have turned into a holiday (for family excursions, spectator sports, etc.), Muslims have imitated the Western weekend.

Feminism

Perhaps the most striking Westernisms fundamentalist Muslims have introduced are associated with women. Taking up the veil and separating women from men may appear to be an archaism, and that's certainly how the fundamentalists see these acts, but it isn't. Fundamentalists actually espouse an outlook more akin to Western-style feminism than anything in traditional Islam. Traditional Muslim men certainly did not take pride in the freedom and independence of their women; but fundamentalists do. Ahmad al-Banna, son of the founder of Egypt's Muslim Brethren, adopts a feminist outlook that leads him to reinterpret Muslim history according to Western standards: "Muslim women have been free and independent for fifteen centuries. Why should we follow the example of Western women, so dependent on their husbands in material matters?"[25]

Traditional Muslim men took pride in their women staying home; in well-to-do households, they almost never left its confines. Hasan at-Turabi has something quite different in mind: "Today in Sudan, women are in the army, in the police, in the ministries, everywhere, on the same footing as men."[26] Turabi proudly speaks of the Islamic movement having helped "liberate women."[27] Following the adage that "the best mosque for women is the inner part of the house,"[28] traditional women prayed at home, and female quarters in mosques were slighted; but fundamentalist women regularly attend public services and new mosques consequently allot far more space to women's sections.

For centuries, a woman's veil served primarily to help her retain her virtue; today, it serves the feminist goal of facilitating a career. Muslim women who wear "Islamic dress," writes a Western analyst,

> are usually well educated, often in the most prestigious university faculties of medicine, engineering, and the sciences, and their dress signifies that although they pursue an education and career in the public sphere, they are religious, moral women. Whereas other women are frequently harassed in the public sphere, such women are honored and even feared. By the late 1980s, Islamic dress had become the norm for middle-class women who do not want to compromise their reputation by their public activities. Boutiques offer Parisian-style fashions adapted to Islamic modesty standards.[29]

The establishment of an Islamic order in Iran has, ironically perhaps, opened many opportunities outside the house for pious women. They do work in the labor force and famously serve in the military. A parliamentary leader boasts, not without reason, about Iran having the best feminist record in the Middle East, and points to the number of women in higher education.[30] In keeping with this spirit, one of Khomeini's granddaughters attended law school and then lived in London with her husband, a cardiac surgeon in training; another organizes women's sporting events.

If the veil used to symbolize a woman's uncontrollable (and therefore destructive) sexuality, fundamentalists see it as the sign of her competence. Turabi declares, "I am for equality between the sexes" and goes on to explain how covering up helps achieve this key feminist goal: "A woman who is not veiled is not the equal of men. She is not looked on as one would look on a man. She is looked at to see if she is beautiful, if she is desirable. When she is veiled, she is considered a human being, not an object of pleasure, not an erotic image."[31]

Curiously, some fundamentalists see the veil representing not careers and equality, but something quite different: positive sexuality. Shabbir Akhtar, a British writer, sees the veil serving "to create a truly erotic culture in which one dispenses with the need for the artificial excitement that pornography provides."[32] Traditional Muslims, it hardly needs emphasizing, did not see veils as a substitute for pornography.

Turning Islam into Ideology

Traditional Islam emphasized man's relations with God while playing down his relations to the state. Law loomed very large, politics small. Over the centuries, pious Muslims avoided the government, which meant almost nothing to them but trouble (taxes, conscription, corvée labor). On the other hand, they made great efforts to live by the *shari'a*.

Infected by the twentieth-century disease, fundamentalists make politics "the heart" of their program.[33] They see Islam less as the structure in which individuals make their lives and more as an ideology for running whole societies. Declaring "Islam is the solution," they hold with Khamenei of Iran that Islam "is rich with instructions for ruling a state, running an economy, establishing social links and relationships among the people and instructions for running a family."[34] For fundamentalists, Islam represents the path to power. As a very high Egyptian official observes, to them "Islam is not precepts or worship, but a system of government."[35] Olivier Roy finds the fundamentalist inspiration to be far more mundane than spiritual: "For many of them, the return to religion has been brought about through their experience in politics, and not as a result of their religious belief."[36]

Revealingly, fundamentalists compare Islam not to other religions but to other ideologies. "We are not socialist, we are not capitalist, we are Islamic," says Anwar Ibrahim of Malaysia.[37] Egypt's Muslim Brethren assert they are neither socialist nor capitalist, but "Muslims."[38] This comparison may seem overblown—socialism and capitalism are universal, fundamentalist Islam limited to Muslims—but it is not, for fundamentalists purvey their ideology to non-Muslims too. In one striking instance, Khomeini in January 1989 sent a letter to Mikhail Gorbachev asserting the universality of Islam. Noting the collapse of communist ideology, he implored the Soviet president not to turn westward for a replacement but to Islam.

> I strongly urge that in breaking down the walls of Marxist fantasies you do not fall into the prison of the West and the Great Satan....I call upon you seriously to study and conduct research into Islam....I openly announce that the Islamic Republic of Iran, as the greatest and most powerful base of the Islamic world, can easily help fill up the ideological vacuum of your system.[39]

As interpreted by a leading Iranian official, this letter "intended to put an end to....views that we are only speaking about the world of Islam. We are speaking for the world."[40] It may even be the case—Khomeini only hints at this—that Islam for him had become so disembodied from faith, he foresaw a non-Muslim like Gorbachev adopting Islamic ways without becoming a Muslim. If so, the transformation of Islam from faith to political construct is then total.

Overhauling the Sacred Law

Even as fundamentalists pay homage to Islam's sacred law, they turn it into a Western-style code and three age-old characteristics of the *shari'a* disappear: its elaboration by independent scholars, its precedence over state interests, and its application to persons, rather than territories.

Developed by the State. Through the centuries, jurists (*faqihs*) wrote and interpreted Islamic law on their own, with little control by governments. The jurists early on established that they were answerable to God, not to the prince. Joseph Schacht, a leading scholar of this subject, explains: "The caliph, though otherwise the absolute chief of the community of Muslims, had not the right to legislate but only to make administrative regulations with the limits laid down by the sacred Law."[41] Rulers did try to dictate terms to jurists but failed. In the years 833-849 C.E., four successive caliphs imposed their understanding of the Qur'an's nature (that it was created by God, as opposed to the religious scholars, who said it had always existed). Despite energetic attempts by the caliphs (which included the flogging of a very eminent religious authority), the effort failed, and with it the pretensions of politicians to define the contents of Islam.

The jurists retained full control of Islamic law until the nineteenth century, when the British, French, and other European rulers codified the *shari'a* as a European-style body of state law. Independent Muslim states, such as the Ottoman Empire, followed the European lead and also codified the *shari'a*. With independence, all the Muslim rulers maintained the European habit of keeping the law firmly under state control; by the 1960s, only in Saudi Arabia did it remained autonomous.

Starting in 1969, Mu'ammar al-Qadhdhafi of Libya started the new wave of expanding the *shar'i* content of state laws (for example, in the criminal statutes). He did so as ruler, using the state apparatus to compel jurists to carry out his orders. Fundamentalist Muslims in many countries then emulated Qadhdhafi, giving the state authority over the *shari'a* even as they extended its purview. They made no effort to revert to the jurists' law of old but continued practices begun by the European powers.

When fundamentalists do on rare occasions protest this state domination of the law, it carries little conviction. Turabi remarks that "Islamic government is not total because it is Islam that is a total way of life, and if you reduce it to government, then government would be omnipotent, and that is not Islam."[42] Turabi's enormous power in the Sudan makes it hard to take this critique seriously. Fundamentalists accept Western ways because, first, they know the imperial system far better than the traditional Muslim one, and so perpetuate its customs. Second, reverting to the traditional Muslim way would, Ann Mayer of the Wharton School points out, "entail that governments relinquish the power that they had gained over legal systems when European-style codified law was originally adopted,"[43] and why should they do that?

State Interests take Priority. The state takeover invariably causes problems. Perhaps most important is that, in the traditional arrangement, the jurists jealously maintained their independence in interpreting the law. They insisted on God's imperatives taking absolute priority over those of the ruler. Such acts as prayer, the fast of Ramadan, or the pilgrimage to Mecca, they insisted, must never be subjected to the whims of despots. Jurists got their way, for hardly a single king or president, not even so

ardent a secularist as Turkey's Kemal Atatürk, had the temerity to interfere with the Lord's commandments.

But Ayatollah Khomeini did. In January 1988, he issued an edict flatly
contravening this ancient Islamic assumption. In a remarkable but little-
noted document, the ayatollah asserted that "the government is authorized unilaterally...to prevent any matter, be it spiritual or material, that
poses a threat to its interests." This means that, "for Islam, the requirements of government supersede every tenet, including even those of
prayer, fasting and pilgrimage to Mecca."[44] Subordinating these acts to
raison d'état has the effect of diminishing the shari'a beyond recognition.

Khomeini—a classical educated scholar, an authority on Islamic law,
and an eminent religious figure—justified this edict on the grounds that
the interests of the Islamic republic were synonymous with the interests
of Islam itself. But this hardly explains so radical and unprecedented a
step. The real reason lies in the fact that, like countless other twentieth-
century rulers, he sought control of his country's spiritual life. Hitler,
Stalin, and Mao subordinated religion to the state, so why not Khomeini?
His edict subordinated Islam to the total state. Khomeini may have looked
medieval but he was a man of his times, deeply affected by totalitarian
ideas emanating from the West. More generally, it had been the case that
only highly qualified jurists could rule on the law. Now anyone with
political power—voter, parliamentarian, or military despot—has potential authority over the outcome. This inevitably leads to the law becoming a tool of state power.

Applies to Geographic Jurisdictions. In traditional Islam (as in
Judaism), laws apply to the individual, not (as in the West) to the territory. It matters not whether a Muslim lives here or there, in the home-
land or in the diaspora; he must follow the shari'a. Conversely, a non-
Muslim living in a Muslim country need not follow its directives. For
example, a Muslim may not drink whisky whether he lives in Tehran or
Los Angeles; and a non-Muslim may imbibe in either place. This leads to
complex situations whereby one set of rules applies to a Muslim thief who
robs a Muslim, another to a Christian who robs a Christian, and so forth.
The key is who you are, not where you are.

In contrast, European notions of law are premised on jurisdictions.
Commit a crime in this town or state and you get one punishment, another in the next town over. Even highways have their own rules. Where

you are, not who you are, is what counts. Ignorant of the spirit underlying the *shari'a*, fundamentalists enforce it along territorial, not personal lines; Turabi declares that Islam "accepts territory as the basis of jurisdiction."[45] As a result, national differences have emerged. The Libyan government lashes all adulterers. Pakistan lashes unmarried offenders and stones married ones. The Sudan imprisons some and hangs others. Iran has even more punishments, including head shaving and a year's banishment.[46] In the hands of fundamentalists, the *shari'a* becomes just a variant of Western, territorial law. This new understanding most dramatically affects non-Muslims, whose millennium-old exclusion from the *shari'a* is over. Now they must live as virtual Muslims. Umar Abd al-Rahman, the Egyptian sheikh in an American jail, is adamant on this subject: "It is very well known that no minority in any country has its own laws."[47] Abd al-Aziz ibn Baz, the Saudi religious leader, calls on non-Muslims to fast during Ramadan. In Iran, foreign women may not wear nail polish—on the grounds that this leaves them unclean for (Islamic) prayer. Entering the country, the authorities provide female visitors with petrol-soaked rags and insist they wipe clean their varnished nails. A fundamentalist party in Malaysia wants to regulate how much time unrelated Chinese men and women may spend alone together.

This new interpretation of Islamic law creates enormous problems. Rather than fairly much leaving non-Muslims to regulate their own conduct, as did traditional Islam, fundamentalism seeks to intrude into their lives, fomenting enormous resentment and sometimes leading to violence. Palestinian Christians who raise pigs find their animals mysteriously poisoned. The million or two Christians living in the northern, predominantly Muslim, region of the Sudan must comply with virtually all the *shar'i* regulations. In the southern Sudan, Islamic law prevails wherever the central government rules, although "certain" *shar'i* provisions are not applied there;[48] should the government conquer the whole south, all the provisions would probably go into effect, an expectation that does much to keep alive a forty-year civil war. Fundamentalist Islam has adopted so many European legal notions that the details may be Islamic but the spirit is Western.

Conclusion: Fundamentalism is Not Transitory

Despite themselves, fundamentalists are Westernizers. Whichever direction they turn, they end up going west. Even in rejecting the West, they accept it. This has two implications. First, however reactionary in intent, fundamentalism imports not just modern but Western ideas and institutions. The fundamentalist dream of expunging Western ways from Muslim life, in short, cannot succeed.

Second, the resulting hybrid is more robust than it seems. Opponents of fundamentalist Islam often dismiss it as a regressive effort to avoid modern life and comfort themselves with the prediction that it is doomed to be left behind as modernization takes place. But this expectation seems mistaken. Because fundamentalism appeals most directly to Muslims contending with the challenges of modernity, its potential grows as does its numbers. Current trends suggest that fundamentalist Islam will remain a force for some time to come. That is not to say that fundamentalism will last, for it will wither just as surely as did the other radical utopian ideologies of this century, fascism and communism. But this process may take decades rather than years, and cause great damage in the process. Opponents of fundamentalism, Muslim or non-Muslim, cannot afford the luxury of sitting back and awaiting its collapse.

NOTES

1. *Al-Sharq al-Awsat*, 17 March 1995.
2. *New York Times*, 4 August 1995.
3. *New York Times*, 5 August 1995.
4. *Le Figaro*, 15 April 1995. Turabi is right that fundamentalist leaders take pride in their knowledge of the West—with the great exception of Ayatollah Khomeini. Symbolic of this lack of curiosity, the dour octogenarian spent almost four months in a suburb of Paris and not once did he set foot in the French capital.
5. Robert H. Pelletreau, Jr., et al., "Symposium: Resurgent Islam in the Middle East," *Middle East Policy* 3, no. 2 (Fall 1994): 20.
6. *New York Times*, 28 July 1995. There he was an active member of the Hamas-backed organization, the United Association for Studies and Research.

7. Hamid Dabashi, *Theology of Discontent: The Ideological Foundations of the Islamic Revolution in Iran* (New York: New York University Press, 1993), 326.

8. Olivier Roy, *Islam and Resistance in Afghanistan* (Cambridge: Cambridge University Press, 1986), 69.

9. Mary Anne Weaver, "Children of the Jihad," *New Yorker*, 12 June 1995. He acknowledges his technical competence in *Al-Hayat*, 12 April 1995; and *Al-Majalla*, 28 May 1995.

10. *New York Times*, 5 August 1995; Radio Monte Carlo, 3 August 1995.

11. *Jerusalem Post*, 21 July 1995.

12. Untitled paper issued by Ramzi in April 1995, starting "My name is ABDUL-BASIT BALOCHI..."

13. Weaver, "Children of the Jihad." Weaver also reports that Ramzi Yusuf's maternal uncle, who is being sought by the Pakistani police for his involvement in fundamentalist violence, served as a regional manager for the Swiss-based charity Mercy International.

14. *Le Figaro*, 15 April 1995.

15. Martin Kramer, "The Jihad against the Jews," *Commentary* (October 1994): 39.

16. *Wall Street Journal*, 22 June 1995.

17. Seyyed Vali Reza Nasr, *The Vanguard of the Islamic Revolution: The Jama'at-i Islami of Pakistan* (Berkeley: University of California Press, 1994), 7-8. For a detailed exposition of Mawdudi's Western orientation, see Seyyed Vali Reza Nasr, *Mawdudi and the Making of Islamic Revivalism* (New York: Oxford University Press, 1996).

18. Shahed Amanullah, *The Minaret* (July-August 1994).

19. Voice of the Islamic Republic of Iran, 4 June 1994.

20. Quoted in François Burgat and William Dowell, *The Islamic Movement in North Africa* (Austin, Tex.: Center for Middle Eastern Studies, University of Texas, 1993), 9.

21. *Shahid* (Farvardin 1369/1990).

22. Detlev H. Khalid [Khalid Duràn], "The Phenomenon of Re-Islamization," *Aussenpolitik* 29 (1978): 448-49.

23. *Oxford Encyclopedia of the Modern Islamic World*, ed. John L. Esposito (New York: Oxford University Press, 1995) [hereafter: *Oxford Encyclopedia*], s.v. "Ulama': Shi'i 'Ulama'" (Shahrough Akhavi), 4:263.

24. S.D. Goitein, *Studies in Islamic History and Institutions* (Leiden: Brill, 1968), 111, n. 1.

25. *Corriere della Sera*, 29 August 1994.

26. *Le Figaro*, 15 April 1995.

27. *Al-Nahar*, 15 July 1995.

28. Tradition quoted by Philip Lewis, *Islamic Britain: Religion, Politics and Identity among British Muslims* (London: Tauris, 1994), 101.

29. *Oxford Encyclopedia*, s.v. "Women and Islam: Women's Religious Observances" (Valerie J. Hoffman-Ladd), 4:327-30.

30. Mohammad Javad Larijani, *Resalat*, 28 June 1995.
31. *Le Figaro*, 15 April 1995.
32. Shabbir Akhtar, *Be Careful With Muhammad! The Salman Rushdie Affair* (London: Bellew Publishing, 1989), 100.
33. Burgat and Dowell, *The Islamic Movement*, 21.
34. Voice of the Islamic Republic of Iran, 7 June 1995.
35. Usama al-Baz, *The Washington Times National Weekly Edition*, 24-30 April 1995.
36. Roy, *Islam and Resistance*, 80.
37. *New York Times*, 28 March 1980.
38. *Al-Ahram Weekly*, 2-8 February 1995.
39. Radio Tehran, 8 January 1989. Khomeini is by no means the only fundamentalist to see the decline of socialism as an opportunity for his favored ideology. Turabi of the Sudan agrees: "Now that socialism has disappeared, there is a great void that only Islam can fill." *La Vanguardia* (Barcelona), 16 July 1995.
40. Mohammad Javad Larijani, *Resalat*, 28 June 1995.
41. Joseph Schacht, *An Introduction to Islamic Law* (Oxford: Clarendon Press, 1964), 53. Those "administrative regulations" in fact amounted to a great deal of law.
42. Quoted in Milton Viorst, "Sudan's Islamic Experiment," *Foreign Affairs* (May-June 1995): 53.
43. Ann Mayer, "The Shari'ah: A Methodology or a Body of Substantive Rules?" in *Islamic Law and Jurisprudence*, ed. Nicholas Heer (Seattle: University of Washington Press, 1990), 182. This discussion relies heavily on Mayer's account.
44. *Keyhan*, 8 January 1988. Nor was this Khomeini's only pronouncement along these lines. For example, shortly after coming to power, he announced that "to serve the nation is to serve God." Radio Tehran, 3 November 1979.
45. Quoted in Judith Miller, "Faces of Fundamentalism: Hassan al-Turabi and Muhammed Fadlallah," *Foreign Affairs* (November-December 1994): 132.
46. Mayer, "The Shari'ah," 193.
47. *New Yorker*, 12 April 1993.
48. Minister of State Ghazi Salah al-Din al-Atabani, quoted in Milton Viorst, "Sudan's Islamic Experiment," 51.

Islamists in Power

Olivier Roy

All Islamist movements advocate a total reshaping of the society along Islamic principles, and see Islam as an encompassing ideology. This constitutes the difference between radical Islamist movements and traditional fundamentalists, who are satisfied with implementation of *shari'a* and Islamic standards of behavior, without caring about the locus of political power. At the same time, Islamist movements embody the social promotion of would-be elites who oppose the traditional elites, including religious hierarchies and the power structures inherited from the post-colonial period. They want to conquer the state in order to establish their new order. In this sense, Islamists are revolutionary.

But they are confronted, once in power, by social, strategic, cultural and economic constraints, and find it difficult to fulfill their promises solely through application of Islamic principles. They have to rely on an increasingly authoritarian and conservative way of ruling, pushing them closer to the traditional fundamentalists, who would rather not be completely bypassed by the "new believers." The shift from a revolutionary movement to a more conservative alliance with traditionalist sectors is a way for recent power to strike roots, but it blurs the line between radical Islam and traditional fundamentalism (as for example in Saudi Arabia). In these cases, Islam in politics serves more as a tool of leverage than as the basis of a new social and political order.

The main predicament of Islamists in power is the contradiction between state logic and *shari'a*. They cast into Islamic terms a political strategy, and dismiss what, in the *shari'a*, might contradict their ideological or strategic approach. In a word, it is the state, or the political power, which defines the place of Islam in an Islamist polity, and not the reverse. Islam is no more for them than a way to legitimize their power and exclude their opponents. This does not mean that Islamists in power do not endeavor to change the society in depth, but the main issues (political system,

Olivier Roy is a research fellow at the Centre National de la Recherche Scientifique, Paris.

economy, social structures) have little to do with Islam proper. Islam as such plays a pivotal role in the legal realm (and specifically the family law), in everyday life (dress, entertainment, public behaviors) and in the symbols of political mobilization (jihad, fatwa). But here two caveats should be made. First, Islamization of law and behaviors has little to do with political Islam. (The Moroccan and Saudi family laws are more "Islamic" than the Iranian laws.) Second, a step presented as "Islamic" may obey a totally different logic, which could just as easily arise from another ideological formula (for example, nationalization of some private properties by the Iranian revolution).

The paradox of political Islam is that if the role of Islam is defined by the state, it means that political power is above any independent religious authority, and thus that Islam is subordinated to politics. And if independent religious authorities control state decisions, that means that there is no such thing as Islamists who exercise absolute power. The paradox disappears only if the highest religious authority is also the highest political leader, something likely to happen only briefly in a revolutionary period. In a word, the distinction between two different levels, religious and political, cannot be bypassed, making impossible an "Islamic totalitarianism" in the true sense of the word.

We will look at Islamists who have held some kind of power in Iran, Afghanistan, Algeria and Turkey. One might immediately object that our examples are very heterogeneous. The only real Islamic revolution is undoubtedly Iran's, but the case of Iran is very specific in the Muslim world, due to the Shiite factor, the existence of a clerical institution, the political alliance of a part of the clerics with "third-worldist" secular intellectuals, and, last but not least, the role played by Iranian nationalism. Many remarks about Iran will not apply to Sunni Islamists, while Iranian ideologues openly dismiss the idea that Sunnism could be the basis for a true Islamic ideology. In contrast, Islamic Afghanistan is nothing but the story of a failed state and regression to segmentation, given a new expression by foreign invasion and civil war. Algerian and Turkish experiences concern only short-term municipal powers (although the Turkish case is rapidly evolving to one of shared national power). Nevertheless, for us, the scarcity and the heterogeneity of Islamists in power are not an accident but the sign of the irrelevance of the concept of Islamism as the new global threat.

Iran: The Tool of Islam

The main feature of Islamic Iran is that the role of Islamic principles is not a given fact but is usually defined by the political power and embodied in written texts, submitted for approbation by popular referendum or vote in the Majlis (parliament). The few exceptions are the fatwas of leading *mujtahids* (religious figures) on some legal questions, and the fatwas of the "guide" *(rahbar)* of the revolution (Khomeini, later Khamenei) on political or more general issues. But by definition these two persons are more politicians than theologians. Whatever the manipulations and pressures, it means that the truly relevant instance is not religious, but political.

Political institutions. The Iranian political framework is a mixture of Western concepts (constitution, revolution, republic, elections, parliament) with Shiite ideological political principles as reshaped by Khomeini *(velayat-e faqih,* or "guardianship of the jurist"). The main originality of the Islamist Iranian political framework, if we compare it with the Sunnis (Egyptian Muslim Brethren or the Jama'at-e Islami of Pakistan), is that it accepts the idea of strictly defined institutions, and does not rely on vague ethical concepts about who the ruler should be and how he should act. The Iranian constitution is not the loosely formulated slogan of the Muslim Brethren ("Qur'an is our constitution"), but is very precise and articulated in line with Western legal concepts (most notably, the separation of powers). The basis of power is both the Iranian nation and the Islamic principles.[1] The national and historical nature of Islamic Iran is thus recognized. The simple idea that the constitution and institutions should be embedded into a national framework introduces concepts totally absent from the *shari'a* and explicitly opposed to the usual political thought among Sunni thinkers: citizenship (vs. "Muslimhood"), state (vs. caliphate), nation (vs. *umma*), etc.

Shiism, as seen by Khomeini, provides an institutional framework which is lacking as far as Sunnis are concerned. In the Shiite tradition, the absence of the twelfth "hidden" Imam allows the religious leaders to rule under his name and to interpret the dogma in pragmatic ways. Islamic law is not a timeless, given corpus, nor is it exclusively defined by a corporation of professional *ulama*, as is normal for Sunni fundamentalists.

It is clear that Islam is not the basis of the whole system. In fact it is the constitution which defines the place of Islam. It is more the law which defines Islam than Islam which defines the law. The affirmation that Islam is the basis of the system is ideological, not juridical. For a true fundamentalist, what is law should be defined by Islam, and not the reverse. The whole Iranian constitutional framework is based on non-Islamic concepts: people's will (Article 1 of the constitution), the nation of Iran, citizenship, elections, separation of powers, obligation for the judge to apply the law of the state, etc. The present constitution could even work for a democratic state with a few amendments (the main one would limit the "guide" to the role of a constitutional monarch).

What is specifically Islamic in the constitution is at the same time specifically Shiite (Article 2 declares that the Imamate is a basic principle of the constitution). This has been further elaborated under the concept of *velayat-e faqih*. The *faqih* concept is conceivable only on the basis of the Shiite theory of the *mujtahid*, that is, the highest religious scholar who has the right to interpret the *shari'a* and becomes the "source of imitation," or *marja'*, for the layman. But it is also an innovation for Shiism. It supposes first that there is only one *marja'* at any one time, whereas the tradition recognizes their collegiality; and second, that the *marja'* should exercise political power directly. But the evolution of the concept after Khomeini's death split the religious aspect from the political one: the endeavor of the Iranian state to push the candidacy of the former president, Khamenei, as the new "guide," is clearly political because he has no religious qualifications for being the sole *marja'*.[2] The religious value of this concept is therefore nullified by a political strategy, which contributes to recreating an autonomous political space around the regime, and an autonomous religious space around the remaining senior clerics who refuse to follow a junior one.

The ambivalence between a political and a religious approach is also to be found in the other institutions. The Council of Guardians *(shura-ye negahbandan)* in charge of controlling the legality of the elections and of the passing of laws is made up of an equal number of clerics and secular lawyers. The Assembly of Experts *(majlis-e khobregan)*, who choose the "guide," is elected by the population, thus leaving the choice of the religiously competent experts to a lay population.

Law and judiciary. In sociological terms, one can speak of an Islamization of the judicial system, but within many limits. The clericalization of the judiciary is compulsory only at the highest level (the head of the Supreme Court and the general prosecutor should be theologians, as should half of the members of the Council of Guardians) and in the special civil courts. If one looks to the passing of laws and the current practices, the picture is not that of the imposition of *shari'a* on the population.

Here also it is the state which defines the role of Islam in the elaboration of law and ruling practice. The law is based on traditional Shiite jurisprudence, except that it is state law. The law is passed by the Majlis (Article 71 of the constitution) and not just interpreted by the judges. In fact, in a true *shari'a* system, nobody should tell the *qadi,* or judge, how to rule. Judging is a non-mediated, direct and totally personal process, whereby the judge uses his knowledge and the handbooks written along the centuries by a chain of scholars, not by the state nor any legislative body. The idea that the law is of divine origin precludes any other systematization than that done by the *ulama,* whatever the time and the space.

In Iran, we do not have the *shari'a,* but a state law partially influenced by the *shari'a.* The main influence of Islam over the law is in matters of personal status. The Special Civil Court Act (September 1979) stated that all family affairs should be deferred to courts headed by religious magistrates, barring attorneys and using informal and direct procedures. The main legal concepts are drawn from *shari'a:* inferiority for women in terms of divorce, allowances and polygamy, and so on.

But even in this field, the sacredness and timelessness of the *shari'a* is easily overlooked for political or social purposes, either by the law itself or through actual court practices. For instance, by law, no divorce is valid without the wife's consent or, in case of dissent, without a court ruling, meaning that the traditional oral practice of *talaq* (repudiation by husband with automatic effect) is not valid in Islamic Iran. Some practices sanctioned by *shari'a* and cast into the law during the first years of the regime, like placing a child in custody of a deceased father's family when his widow remarries, have antagonized public opinion because of the number of martyrs' widows in the aftermath of the war with Iraq. Before his death, Khomeini issued a statement allowing these widows to retain custody over their children. Although this is not a change in the general law, it indicates that the *shari'a* is prone to a pragmatic and political reading.

In the late 1980s, the government introduced a new standard marriage contract which gives women more rights than allowed by the *shari'a* (the legal justification being that *shari'a* acknowledges contracts). Thus, feminist public opinion is acknowledged without formally giving up the *shari'a*. In December 1991, the government also passed a law which recognizes fictional wages for housework, thus allowing compensation for a divorced wife, another way to bypass both the letter and the spirit of the traditional *shari'a*, which limits post-divorce allowances to three months. The evolution of Iranian women's rights since 1980 shows that the government had to change the law several times in order to give more rights to women. A study of actual court rulings shows that the usual court practice is to bend the *shari'a* in favor of women, although the basic inequality between men and women is not put into question.[3] Such rulings in Iran are more favorable to women than rulings in "conservative" Morocco and Egypt (not to speak of Saudi Arabia), where a man can unilaterally divorce his wife without any formal ruling of the court.

These studies shows that this relatively "feminist" bias is a consequence both of the strength of Iranian society, where women are traditionally more powerful than in Arab societies, and of the political will of the regime not to appear misogynous. Limits of Islamization are clearly sociological and political. Iran shows that even for "Islamic states," *shari'a* is not carved in stone and can be adapted to the political and social environment.

But such a system, based on a dual legitimacy (state and *shari'a*), is not stable. There are many contradictions and much overlapping between *shari'a* and state law. If judges are requested to apply the state law, they might, in some non-political cases, take into account specific fatwas if asked by one party. They also might refuse to apply the state law if it is in contradiction with Islam (Article 170 of the constitution), although they are nevertheless requested first to rule according to the law (Article 167), in order to avoid personal interpretation. Such discrepancy and incoherence usually lead to legal stalemates, because authorities would prefer not to make a choice which might highlight the fact that the state law is not really Islamic and cannot become truly Islamic.

On other legal points that are pivotal to the traditional Sunni approach to the *shari'a*, Iranian law has nothing to do with *shari'a*. One example is citizenship and the status of *dhimmis* (non-Muslim believers). Members of religious minorities in Iran are citizens. They are drafted into the army and do not pay special taxes, although they have their own constituencies for elections and no Muslim can be executed for killing a Christian. The law of citizenship has nothing to do with Islam: a Persian-speaking Afghan Shiite resident in Iran faces tremendous difficulties if he wishes to be naturalized, to own land, or to marry an Iranian woman. The precedence of citizenship over "Muslimhood" became obvious when Jellaluddin Farsi, an Islamist Shiite ideologue, born in Iran and an Iranian citizen, was barred in 1982 from running for president, because his father was Afghan.

The economy. The so-called "Islamic economy" in Iran is in fact a third-world statist economy inspired by leftist ideology, coupled with a tradition of the rentier state, and cloaked in Islamic legal rhetoric. From 1980 to 1989, Islam was invoked to legitimize a statist policy, especially nationalizations and confiscations of private properties in favor of foundations (*bonyads*), which benefitted the client networks of the ruling elites. Opposition to this redistribution, stressing the right to property, was also expressed in an Islamic idiom.

As far as the banking system is concerned, prohibition of interest simply led to its reformulation as risk sharing, usually by prohibiting fixed interest but virtually assuring some other form of profit. Some of these reformulations include interest-free accounts, for which the bank provides non-interest incentives for the customer; term certificates of deposit, in which customers and banks share the risks and profits; and investment partnerships, either on an equal footing *(mosharekat)* or joint ventures where the bank can sell its shares.

Some changes were made regarding real property (the separation of ownership of land and the buildings on it), religious endowments (*waqf* have been fully restored), and so on. But when the question of *waqf* contradicted the policy of helping the "deprived" (for example, by restoring religious *waqf* on lands bought by peasants at the time of the Shah's "White Revolution" in 1963), the question has been symbolically resolved by a token rent. Usually conservatism prevailed and little changed.[4] Article 45 of the constitution extends state property by invoking the supposed restriction on private ownership of *mawat* or non-cultivated land. This is clearly a political interpretation of the *shari'a*, because the state is supposed to act in the name of the community. As the concept of the state is absent from the *shari'a*, it is clear that we have here an "Islamic" formulation of a statist, leftist policy. These new rules did not drastically change economic relations, but permitted a new elite to get perks and redistribute some wealth among its constituency.

Islamic economic principals are not applied to transactions with foreign countries. When economic reforms were undertaken from 1989 (through Mohsen Nourbakhsh, minister of economy; Mohammed Adeli, governor of the Central Bank; and Masud Roghani-Zanjani, minister of plan and budget), there was no attempt to explain them in Islamic terms. The logic here has nothing to do with Islam, but with the IMF and World Bank. As a consequence, most of the positive social actions in favor of the deprived have been dropped and the living standards of the bulk of the population have drastically fallen. The rearguard combat against reforms is mainly aimed at maintaining the rentier state and the speculative role of the bazaar. Such reform as exists is justified less and less in Islamic terms.

On the social level, Islamization has also been a cloak for progressivist action in the countryside, through the "Reconstruction Jihad," which had some positive results but no real effect on re-Islamization of the countryside. In fact, this is the only real "progressive" action of a revolution that claimed it would bring prosperity to the deprived. The real effect has been to extend state influence to a countryside which stood aloof from the revolution. In cities, the social effects of the various foundations became no more than a way to distribute perks among the regime's constituents, mainly to the *nouveaux riches*.

Such a key social and economic issue as land reform was debated, from 1981 to 1984, in terms of interest groups. (Khomeini refused to take sides, which would have been rather strange had the debate been about Islam.) Only when the political decision to give up the reform was taken, did the authorities sometimes express their position in Islamic terms.[5]

Customs and way of life. The main change brought by the Islamic revolution outside the political sphere has been in daily life, external behaviors, and culture. The mandatory *hijab* is the most obvious and obnoxious constraint. Restrictions on clothing and coeducation hurt mainly the middle class, which cannot stand the rigorous social control but cannot afford the costly ways of escaping censorship. The main victims are women, but also youth in search of entertainment. Strangely enough, several forms of art, and particularly films, do flourish, although the *hijab* imperative limits many movies to children or hospital stories.

Traditional culture has been threatened but saved, as shown by classical Persian music, first condemned, then rehabilitated as part of the "national Iranian heritage." Publishing of new books and translations is thriving. The "moral order" remains superficial, although pervasive.

In fact, modern Iranian society has not been destroyed. There is a new elite, but clericalization of the society has been limited, not only by the passive resistance of the population, but also because the bulk of the clergy is increasingly determined not to be identified with a failing regime and economy, as shown by the attitude of Ayatollah Mohammed Montazeri (formerly Khomeini's heir apparent) and many leading ayatollahs. The losers are the modern intelligentsia, the salaried middle class, and the entrepreneurial class.

It is obvious that in Iran, Islam is an ideological tool in the hands of a new power structure, which has its own agenda: to remain in power, but also to promote Iranian national interests in the Middle East.

Algeria and Turkey: The Municipal Experience

During the municipal elections of June 1990, the Islamic Salvation Front (FIS) captured twenty-eight of the thirty largest municipalities. It had no time to change local life in depth. The action of the Islamist municipalities turned first on symbols: renaming streets and public offices, putting green flags and Islamic slogans everywhere. The second level was well-publicized social actions: "Islamic markets" at low prices for primary goods (meat and bread, but also school books and tools). In attempting to change economic and social conditions, city councils redistributed the perks traditionally allotted by the Algerian system to the different strata of power-holders. City councils are entitled to distribute rented apartments, building permits, allotments of land for social estates, trading licenses and municipal jobs. In the hands of the Islamists, this action turned very rapidly into a new clientelism.

Islamic municipalities also worked promote "morality" and "decent dress" within their boundaries. They encouraged women (specially city employees) to wear the veil, and they prohibited short pants for men (through a city council's edict in Tibasa for example). The Oran municipality forbade a *rai* festival (*rai* is a form of popular and secular music, born in Oran). But it soon became apparent that the Islamist municipal policies simply shifted favors from one patron-client network to another, explaining the decrease in FIS votes in the December 1990 legislative elections.

Turkey's Refah city councils have operated under the same constraints as their FIS counterparts, although they are more professional, trained and politically minded. They have adopted a lower political profile and have played more on honesty and efficiency than on symbols and morality. They have acted more cautiously, but with the same agenda. The Istanbul city council tried to ban alcohol in the sidewalk restaurants and cafes so characteristic in the scenic parts of the city, but they had to retreat in the face of a counter-offensive from businessmen and restaurant owners. Female municipal employees are authorized and encouraged to wear "Islamic dress." On the cultural level, the city councils are more reticent in promoting "Muslim culture" (it is difficult to speak of Islamic dance and music). Instead they promote a sort of "Ottoman culture," mixing Turkish nationalism, Muslim heritage, and "decency." Here also, emphasis on national identity supersedes a purely Islamic one.

City councils are thwarted in their efforts by state law. For example, when the Konya municipality tried to organize alternative public transportation for women only, it was threatened by a suit before the constitutional court, for violating citizens' equality. But they are also able to use censorship tools established by their social-democrat predecessors (such as the city committee for arts in Istanbul).

The main asset of the Refah city councils is their image of efficiency and honesty. But they might also be tempted to play on the same logic of clientelism as their predecessors, thus identifying "Islam" with a specific constituency, not with "the people." On the other hand, if they maintain a technocratic profile and avoid the promotion of Islamic symbols, they might lose some of their constituents to more radical groups.

Afghanistan: The Failed State

There are no "Islamic institutions" in the political field, but there is the sheer exercise of power by military commanders, on the basis of traditional solidarity groups reshaped by almost twenty years of wars and revolutions.

Shari'a is not an instrument of state policy but is imposed, by local mullahs, on areas of life where there is no political stake or interference from the local armed commanders. There has been a total collapse of the judiciary. When a political group advocates *shari'a*, it does so to legitimize itself against the state—not only against the existing weak government, but against the very idea of a state. In this sense, promotion of *shari'a* does not work in favor of a clerical establishment, but of "solidarity groups" (*qawm*), based on personal links, tribalism, ethnicity—and guns (e.g., the Taleban movement). For the Taleban, the *"shari'a only"* motto is also a way to ignore the question of the ethnic nature of power; they are all Pashtuns, and their refusal to share power with Burhanuddin Rabbani, expressed on Islamic grounds, is also a way to reestablish traditional Pashtun supremacy. In May 1996, the Taleban called for a consultation (*shura*) in Kandahar that elected their leader as *amir al-mu'minin*, that is head of all the Muslims, and called for a jihad against the present head of state, Rabbani. The only snag is that Rabbani has as many Islamic credentials, if not more, than any Taleban leader.

The present government (led by Rabbani and Ahmad Shah Masud since 1993) is also very vague about implementing *shari'a*: it lets local mullahs, courts and armed commanders rule as they want. But it also allows women to work and to go out of their houses, and the state employs many women. The economy is totally free; drug trafficking flourishes, notwithstanding the various fatwas declaring it illegal. Taleban systematically take charge in schools and courts, but do not interfere with social life. The government did not drastically alter the curriculum of the government schools, and did not even bother to change some symbols (such as postage stamps, which are the same ones used under the communists).

In fact, Islam is rhetorical and the political game operates without any Islamic reference: the Taleban who brand the Azhar-trained Rabbani "un-

Islamic" were once allied with Abdurrashid Dustom, a former communist and present imbiber of alcohol.

Plus la même chose

Islamists in power do change many basic aspects of society, in a short span
of time and by using spectacular or even violent means (such as destruction of liquor stores, enforcing of the veiling of women, executions of
opponents). But, violence apart, the final results are not very different of
what we see in more conservative Muslim countries. The Islamists do not
create a new kind of totalitarian system. Their main mark on the society
is Islamization according to patterns similar to those of conservative and
pro-Western states like Saudi Arabia (veil, ban on alcohol, restriction on
coeducation and entertainments, and so on.). They are even rather more
"democratic" than many other conservative Middle Eastern regimes.
(Most notably, there are elections in Iran, although restricted to "Islamic"
groups.) What really separates them, in Western eyes, from the Saudi
establishment, is their foreign policy: they are anti-Western, they oppose
the Arab-Israeli peace process, and they support radical groups abroad.
In fact, radicalism remains a constant in foreign policy, not in domestic
policy.

But even in foreign policy, the Islamists in power are limited by strategic and national constraints. They simply express in ideological terms
what is clearly a nationalist policy: the Iranian regime, the Algerian FIS
and the Refah party in Turkey, as well as the Palestinian Hamas and even
the Lebanese Hizbullah, increasingly cast their strategy in terms of national interests. They became "Islamo-nationalists," giving up any idea
of building up the *umma* beyond their own nation.

In some aspects of law and society, Islamists in power might even be
less "Islamic" than conservative states. For example, family law is less
restrictive against women in Iran than in Morocco, and the penal code is
less "Islamic" than in Saudi Arabia. Religious practices, like prayers, are
not enforced by a special police in Iran as they are in Saudi Arabia. In all
these aspects, Saudi Arabia is more "Islamic" than Iran or even Afghanistan (where there are films, music, and dance). Paradoxically, Islamization
does not characterize Islamists in power. What is new is the call for an

overall Islamic society, including politics and economy—in a word, the ideologization of Islam. This ideologization is visible in the systematic us of Islamic symbols (slogans, pictures, Qur'anic verses, *bismillah* to introduce any official statements). But when one goes to the basic tenets of the society (politics, economy and social relations), the picture changes.

In politics, Islam is, for Islamists, an ideological tool to maintain their power. Islam, once turned into an ideology, can be bent at will to legitimize state policy. Hence the different colors of Islamization: it might be statist or it might favor a private economy; it might exclude women from public life (the Taleban in Afghanistan) or promote a kind of "Islamic freedom" for them (Iran); it might strike a deal with the Christians (Iran), or call for their expulsion. There is no one "Islamic ideology," but there are different "Islamic" readings of different social and political attitudes— readings shaped by power politics. Reference to Islam also provides a criterion to dismiss political opponents. The myth of the *umma* works to disqualify those who would "divide" the community. This leverage can be easily manipulated because the Islamists are always the first to dismiss the legitimacy of any independent religious authority, in order to be the only ones to speak in the name of "true Islam." (In Iran, for example, the Islamic regime worked hard to shunt aside or isolate all the *marja*'s except Ayatollah Khomeini.)

This flexibility looks like opportunism. One of the consequences is that Islam loses its power of mobilization as soon as it is identified with a specific group. Society then either heads towards a kind of secularization by disillusion, or towards the restoration of an independent, apolitical Islamic pole, which challenges the pretension of the regime to embody Islam. Both trends are obvious in Iran: on the one hand religious practice is decreasing, on the other hand some clerics (Montazeri) or lay thinkers (Abdolkarim Sorush) call for a distinction between Islam and state.

Ultimately, Islamists in power do not meet the expectations of the population. Corruption returns, the economic situation worsens, politics is little more than a factional struggle for power, women are unhappy about the limitations on social life and job opportunity, young people are left with few entertainments. The answer cannot be the mere suppression of any opposition.

The Islamist Contradiction

Even if the Islamist regimes are authoritarian and coercive, why is there no "Islamic totalitarianism"? My answer is that there is a contradiction in Islamist ideology. If it does respect the basic idea of the *shari'a*, it cannot control the family and has to admit the existence of a private sphere beyond the reach of the state. If it does not respect the *shari'a*, then this ideology might be opposed in the very name of Islam.

In fact, we have two different, if not contradictory, logics. There is the logic of the *shari'a*, based on casuistry, on a case-by-case approach, on an autonomous development of corpus, hostile to any written systematization through an all-encompassing code and to any legislative action by a state or parliament. And there is the logic of the state, seeking to use the law in order to implement a specific policy. True *shari'a* would mean devolution of law from the state to the religious courts. But the Islamist state never gives up its lawmaking power in favor of *shari'a*. That could happen only where there is no state. Afghanistan most closely approximates this situation, and even there, politics interfere.

The duality of state law and *shari'a* is still the predicament of the elusive Islamic state. By definition, *shari'a* defines a private space *(haram)* which the state cannot penetrate. Family as such should not be touched. And how can a state be totalitarian if it recognizes the family's untouchable status? The question arose in revolutionary Iran during the 1980s. How could a house search be made religiously legal, if it resulted in a young man seeing a *haram* woman? This question is surely rhetorical in terms of police practices, but not in terms of legitimacy. In this instance, coercive action from the state appears as outright illegitimate. Khomeini himself had to regularly address the question, and house searches are rather limited nowadays.

Compared with communism, Islamism has less leverage to change the society from above. There is the basic fact of social acceptance or resistance to Islamization. Conservative societies (like Morocco and Afghanistan) more readily accept a very Islamic family law, even when it is not imposed by the state in the name of Islamization, while more modern and sophisticated societies, like Iran, oblige the state to water down its commitment or issue more flexible rulings, as we saw in the case of divorce. It is easier to ban driving for women, as well as music, in Saudi Arabia than in Iran. When it comes to law and family status, radical political Islamists are not necessarily more "Islamic" than traditional and pro-Western elites.

The dualist approach ("bad Islamists" against "good secularists") misses the point about the real changes in contemporary Muslim societies. Islamization cannot work as an abstract practice that ignores actual society. The need to achieve some consensus and to play on nationalism obliges the Islamists to accept a certain degree of cultural specificity. Cultural and sociological factors (the role of women, urbanization, passage from extended to nuclear families, education) are more important than the explicit ideology of the rulers. For instance, it is not by chance that the issue of the veil is pivotal in societies which experienced a brutal modernization with the coming of women into the labor market (Iran, Algeria, France for immigrants), while it remains secondary in more traditional societies (Afghanistan, Pakistan, Morocco).

I will not enter here into the question whether the Islamist movement is a backlash against modernization, or an agent of modernization.[6] But it should be stressed that Islamism is helpless against long-term sociological evolutions—urbanization, Westernization, expanded role of women—which will undermine the basic tenets of its ideology. Whatever judgement we pass on Islamism, it will not survive the test of actual rule—and it will fail faster than communism.

NOTES

1. The preamble explicitly states that the constitution has been accepted by the Iranian nation by a majority of 98.2 percent, which roots the constitution in the political will of the nation, not the Muslim *umma* (Christians were also voters).
2. See Shaul Bakhash, "Iran: The Crisis of Legitimacy," *Middle Eastern Lectures* 1(1995): 99-118. *Ed.*
3. For an in-depth analysis of laws and court practices in Iran (compared with Morocco), see Ziba Mir-Hosseyni, *Marriage on Trial* (London: Tauris, 1993); see also Homa Hoodfar, "Women and Personal Status Law in Iran," an interview with Mehranguiz Kar, in *Middle East Report*, no. 198 (January 1996).
4. See Mehrdad Haghayeghi, "Agricultural Development Planning under the Islamic Republic of Iran," *Iranian Studies* 23, nos. 1-4 (1990): 5-29.
5. Ibid., 9.
6. See Olivier Roy, *The Failure of Political Islam* (Cambridge: Harvard University Press, 1994).

DISCUSSION

David Menashri (Tel Aviv University): Certainly there are some contradictions in the Iranian constitution, but to say that it is not Islamic is pushing the argument a bit too far. How do you explain the Iranian constitution investing so much authority in the *faqih*, even after the 1989 amendment of the constitution? Or the Council of Guardians, which has to approve all legislation based at least in part on Islamic rulings?

Olivier Roy: I did not say that the Iranian constitution is not Islamic. I said that it is the state which decides what is Islamic in it. The last word is political, not religious. And if we look at the institutions, this is how it actually works. For example, half of the Council of Guardians is appointed by the "guide," half by the parliament. The "guide" himself also depends on the Assembly of Experts, which is elected by the population. There is no escape from politics.

David Menashri: Nonetheless, it only requires a majority of the six members of the Council of Guardians appointed by the "guide" to veto any legislation that contradicts Islam. Whereas it requires a majority of all twelve together to veto legislation which contradicts the constitution.

Olivier Roy: Absolutely. But my point is that Islam is not the last word as such. Islam is a political tool used by the different players against opponents and of course against each other. But in the end it is the political calculation which is decisive. Contrary to what the true Islamists would have liked, Islam does not rule. It is human beings, political actors, who rule. Islam doesn't provide a third way between Western capitalism and communism, it is not a consistent system, and it is contingent on political, strategic, social, economic, and even cultural constraints.

We cannot drop the word Islam, the concept of Islam, when we study Iran today. It is more than just window-dressing. But the underlying explanation lies in politics—the political game between different groups, using Islam to prop themselves up and inflict damage upon one another.

Participant: If the Iranian regime has abandoned ideology in almost every field, then how do you explain Iran's anti-Israeli position? Is this a fig leaf to cover up their abandonment of ideology in all other fields?

Olivier Roy: Islam is not just a fig leaf, it is at least a fig tree. They need to root their legitimacy in something. President Rafsanjani simply cannot say that he is following this or that policy "because I am a pragmatist." He has to say, "I am an Islamist pragmatist," because there are many more people in Iran who are prepared to be far more pragmatic than he is. The regime cannot give up its Islamic legitimation. But since Islam is withdrawing from most fields, they must maintain Islamic pretenses at some symbolic level. In terms of foreign policy, they do so in two arenas: the Arab-Israeli peace process and the Rushdie affair. The problem for them is that neither of these causes has any appeal among the population. Nor do they articulate the interests of the country or the state. They simply help to legitimate a weak regime.

Should the West Promote Rights or *Realpolitik?*

Europe can't do either, argues Claire Spencer: it has no coherent policy, and maybe it shouldn't, given the diversity of the Islamist "challenge." Not good enough for a great power, claims Robert Satloff: the United States has Muslim friends and interests, and must defend them. Perhaps, answers Ann Elizabeth Mayer, but if the West is going to talk about human rights too, it should employ one standard—or see its influence wane.

Europe and Political Islam: Defining Threats and Evolving Policies

Claire Spencer

It is a relatively uncontroversial, if rarely stated truth, that there is no such thing as a European policy towards Islam or Islamism. It might even be said that there is no such thing as "European policy" towards all but the most general of foreign policy objectives, if even then a consensus holds among European governments.

This is not for want of trying. As is well-known, in the Maastricht Treaty concluded by member-states of the European Union, an aspiration exists under the treaty's Title V, Article J4 to create what is termed a Common Foreign and Security Policy (CFSP) for the European Union (EU) as a whole.[1] It is also not entirely true to say that Europeans have been "sleeping through the night" in the face of important foreign policy decisions or actions, as has been alleged by certain of Europe's transatlantic colleagues, or at least by one much-quoted colleague in particular.[2]

Europe's Foreign Policy Quandary

But there are two basic problems associated with the evolution of European policies. The first stems from institutional limitations. The European Commission, which is the central bureaucracy of the EU, has very little competence in this area, beyond the elaboration of ministerial decisions. European foreign policy evolves through discussion at the interministerial level, or the "intergovernmental pillar" of the EU. Given the need for consensus, the kind of foreign policy statements which emerge after ministerial meetings on issues relating to foreign affairs tend to be at the level of generalities or statements of good intent. These statements cannot in any way be considered binding on individual members of the European Union, especially when it comes to joint actions envisaged by fewer than

Claire Spencer is is the deputy director of the Centre for Defence Studies, King's College, University of London.

the total of fifteen EU members. Despite the aspirations of a number of EU states, the evolution of the common European project has not yet reached what might be termed a "United States of Europe," nor is this even an eventuality to which all EU-member states are committed.

The second constraint to coherent policy lies in the sphere of military action. If one considers political Islam or its more radical manifestations as a threat to European security in any way, European governments are constrained in actions which go beyond the defense of their immediate national interests, by their membership in international defensive alliances. These include the Western European Union (which one sometimes has the impression only Europeans have heard of), but most importantly, the North Atlantic Treaty Organization (NATO), which engages non-European members, and above all the United States. The recent missions of European military establishments, whether in peacekeeping in Bosnia, or in the Gulf war and subsequent sanctions against Iraq, have all required at very least the acquiescence of the U.S. (if only initially as a "sleeping" or passive partner) in the planning and execution of European policy.

Since March 1996, the EU has been engaged in an Inter-Governmental Conference (IGC) to review the development of the CFSP, among other aspects of the implementation of the Maastricht Treaty. It has been proposed to create the post of a spokesperson for European foreign policy, along the lines of the EU representative appointed to oversee the Dayton Treaty's process in the former Yugoslavia. For more general purposes, this suggestion has yet to be further developed, not least because of the relatively limited objectives of the CFSP within the Maastricht Treaty. The wording of the relevant Maastricht article concentrates less on its broader foreign and security aspects than on "the eventual framing of a common defense policy, which might lead in turn to a common defense."[3]

The hope of some EU member states is that this in turn might lead to the eventual formation of a European army. However, at least four EU members are neutral states (Finland, Austria, Sweden and Ireland). Not all states have professional armies, nor compatible bases on which to build a common European army. Not all states have the same constitutional freedoms to engage in operations beyond national defense, nor (once again) do they have the same degree of political consensus to engage with other European partners in joint activities. Thus, for example, while Germany and France have formed the basis of a combined "Eurocorps," it was Britain and France which sent the majority of European forces to the former Yugoslavia, the direct engagement of German troops being limited by Germany's historical role in the Balkans.

For the foreseeable future, European states will continue to hold on to the preeminence of national governments and national parliaments in the formation and articulation of foreign policy. This is because the safeguarding of national sovereignty and national competence in both internal and external affairs is one of the most hotly disputed areas in negotiations over the future shape of the European Union.

Europe, Islam and Islamism

The relevance of the constraints outlined above is most keenly felt in areas where there is no consensus over external military threats to European security. This is especially salient when one looks at European approaches, attitudes and policies towards Islamism and Islamist movements. Only at the extremes of policy-making establishments are they perceived to constitute a potential military threat to Europe's existence. Rather, the threat of terrorist activity has been uppermost in the minds of European governments, inspiring active cooperation between Britain, France and Germany, for example, in intelligence-sharing and the extradition of Algerian Islamists linked to the bomb attacks in Paris and Lyons in the summer of 1995.

The control of terrorism nevertheless generally continues to pertain to the sphere of national defense, and goes beyond the question of Islamism and Islamist radicals alone. Combatting the IRA in Britain and ETA in Spain has given both states considerable experience in this field. However, European cooperation over terrorism depends on reaching common views on the sources of violent activity and the identification of terrorist suspects. A minor dispute arose recently between Spain and Belgium, for example, over the latter's refusal to deport two ETA suspects for judgment in the Spanish courts.

Over more general instances of Islamist activism, is it possible for more to be achieved, or at least coordinated at the European level? There are four areas of difficulty associated with this. The first lies in defining the nature of the "Islamist problem," as well as how and by whom this is to be judged. This is an issue which not only arises between states, where, for example, France is more directly affected by the crisis in Algeria, but also within states. In Britain, for example, tensions have arisen between the Home Office and the Foreign and Commonwealth Office over asylum cases involving Islamist activists which may affect relations with third states. The case of the Tunisian Islamist opposition leader, Rashid al-Ghannushi, who was accorded asylum in the U.K. in the late 1980s, has continued to sour U.K.-Tunisian relations well into the 1990s. In other words, a decision made independently by interior ministry officials may continue to complicate the lives of foreign ministry officials well beyond the circumstances and rationale of the original asylum case.

Another more recent example of this arose over the case of the Saudi dissident-in-exile in Britain, Muhammad al-Mas'ari. The debate over whether this vehement Islamist opponent of the Saudi regime should be granted a more permanent leave to stay in the U.K. went well beyond a discussion of policy towards political Islam. The problem began with an indirect request from the Saudi authorities for al-Mas'ari's application for political asylum to be turned down, the implication being that his presence in Britain was damaging for the U.K.'s commercial and political relations with Saudi Arabia.

The case provoked two reactions and some unusual alliances. On the one hand were those who aligned against the infringement of British sovereignty which would be implied if the British government bowed to Saudi pressure. On the other hand were those who spoke in defense of the British jobs which would be lost if the Saudi government were to cancel any existing trade agreements, and especially defense contracts, with British companies. The first alliance brought together what is often called the "Jolly England brigade," a loose coalition of opponents of any external influence, European or other, over matters decided in London, with a number of human rights groups. The second group of free-traders and commercial groups argued from the principle of the greater good —namely the employment and well-being of many in Britain—against the potential damage to be wrought by one individual.

Ultimately, Mas'ari's right to stay in Britain was decided by the courts. The case nevertheless illustrates the difficulty of separating one area of policy from another where a number of interests—especially national and international security—are at stake.

Islamism and Security

At heart, however, the preoccupation with Islamism is a security concern. In early 1995, the erstwhile secretary-general of NATO, Willy Claes, made a well-reported gaffe when he identified Islamism as the greatest threat to Western security following communism. Even though it was accepted that his comments were taken out of context, individual NATO member governments swiftly dissociated themselves from this broad and damaging allusion. In the minds of many European policy-makers is the possible impact of policies towards Islamists on Muslim communities resident within European states. As a result, most governments are at pains to distinguish between the religious and cultural heritage of Islam, and its use to political ends. The fact that this is not always clearly stated, or is misrepresented in the media, means that sensitivities are often aroused when allusions to security concerns are made.

This is not to say that much progress has been made by European governments in pinpointing the real nature of the concern with Islamist activism. In reality, it tends to arise where domestic and foreign policies intersect, such as in the sensitive areas of visa, asylum and migration policies which have yet to be well-coordinated at the European Union level.

In this respect, the second challenge to coherent European policy-making lies precisely where the internal and external impacts of Islamist activism come together. This is particularly clear in the case already cited of France and Algeria, where a large population of Algerians and French citizens of Algerian descent resides on French soil, and where France has particularly strong historical, economic and political ties with Algeria. In the later years of Mitterrand's presidency, this gave rise to the unusual spectacle of French policy towards Algeria being directed concurrently, and occasionally at cross purposes, by the minister of the interior, Charles Pasqua, the then-foreign minister, Alain Juppé, and by the presidency and Prime Minister Balladur's office. Official utterances by one minister, such as Pasqua's condemnation of Algerian Islamists, were tempered by the initiatives of others, such as President Mitterrand's proposal in early 1995 to host an international conference, which was subsequently played down by the foreign ministry.

Because of these domestic ramifications, other European governments have been reluctant to evolve independent policy approaches to the Algerian crisis for fear of arousing French sensibilities. In some instances, the French government has put pressure on its European partners to conform to policies already adopted in Paris. British Foreign Office officials, for example, have fallen into line with their French counterparts in refusing to engage in discussions with members of the Algerian Islamic Salvation Front (or FIS), the main (but officially banned) Islamist opposition to the military-backed government of Algeria.

This relates to the third problem, namely the varying levels of interest and concern within European states over the security implications of Islamist radicalism. Different states are affected by different types of Islamist movements in different ways and at different times. For example, Germany's preoccupation has been with events in Turkey and the broader Middle East rather more than in North Africa. Within Germany's Muslim/Turkish migrant communities, tensions have arisen over Kurdish activism and the rise of German racism towards Turks in general, neither of which is strictly related to broader Islamist questions. In Germany's bilateral relations with France, however, the presence as a political refugee in Germany of the FIS activist, Rabah Kebir, has led to a number of tensions, especially when Kebir has used the French press to be critical of France's policy towards Algeria. As a result of such incidents, the German government has periodically cautioned Kebir to silence.

In southern Europe, Spain's preoccupation is largely with events in Morocco, and particularly with migrant pressures across the Mediterranean, as is Italy's concern with Tunisia and Libya. Both states have been perceived as potential transit states for migrants, Islamists and terrorists (the three groups being frequently confused) moving further north. As the internal borders of the EU have moved towards looser controls in recent years, especially for those EU states that have signed the Schengen accords (namely, France, Germany, Spain, Portugal, Italy and the Benelux countries), frictions between EU countries over the free movement of peoples may also stand to increase.

Although the basic principle of Schengen—namely, common border controls—has yet to be fully applied beyond an initial trial period, it remains the case that once an individual has passed an external EU border into Spain, for example, he or she might just as well be in Bonn, since no barriers will exist to prevent him or her moving there. If by this time no common position has evolved over the relative security risks presented by individual Islamists, then further frictions between EU members may arise.

In the U.K., concerns over Islamist extremism stretch beyond the Middle East to the potential engagement of Muslims from the Indian subcontinent in radical groups, as has been seen in the activities of the Hizb al-Tahrir movement, active in British university circles frequented by a number of British Asians. However, the antisemitic and other inflammatory statements of Hizb al-Tahrir make this movement less susceptible to control through a coherent policy towards Islamist activism than through existing legislation on race relations and incitement to racial hatred. The group is also not well supported among the broader British Muslim community. As far as foreign policy is concerned, the case of Salman Rushdie remains a major preoccupation, particularly in attempts to regularize relations with Iran, which are in stalemate while the death threat to Rushdie continues.

The fourth problem is in a sense a culmination of the others, namely the difficulties attendant on elaborating European policy towards something as broad as Islamism, definitions of which detain even the most astute of researchers and academics in the field. For practical purposes, most governments prefer to deal with individual asylum-seekers, Islamist groups and foreign opposition movements on a case-by-case basis. Given the complexities of what may be at stake—political and social, as well as economic—this is usually what is most appropriate or as much as can be hoped for.

The danger arises when a whole series of security concerns are mixed together, regardless of the relative weight of a potential security threat or the likelihood of that potential threat becoming a reality. Too frequently, Europeans participate in public debates on migration, visa and asylum policies which make direct links to Islamist-inspired violence. Consequently, the general issues associated with the free movement of Muslims within Europe are particularized by the activities of a very small minority from within, or often alien to, Muslim communities in Europe. The case of al-Mas'ari highlighted the problem in Britain, in which the case of one individual re-ignited existing debate over the access to the

U.K. of potentially disruptive opponents of Britain's major trading partners, many of whom come from Muslim countries.

In the context of such debates, it is extremely difficult to isolate Islamism or the Islamist component of a challenge or policy debate from the rest of the issues. In fact, embarking on a discussion of one issue tends to unleash all the rest, especially if the issue concerns the overspill effects in Europe of violence or political disruption on Europe's borders, as in the case of Algeria. While the rise of Islamist activism in London may initially be seen as a potential problem for the U.K., it soon becomes a problem for the rest of Europe if a network of links are found to exist between Islamist activists in one or more of the capitals of Europe. Despite the evident need for a minimum level of policy coordination, one still needs to ask whether it is possible to talk of evolving a common European policy towards Islamism, and whether it is even desirable.

Europe, Islamism and Mediterranean Security

Unlike the U.S. government, European governments have made few serious attempts to distinguish between moderate and extremist Islamists, or even to establish criteria for doing so. In Britain, the pragmatic "case study" approach is adopted, not only because of the different levels of national and international interests at stake, but also because of the complexities of speculating on what Islamist groups would or would not do if they were to take power in the states whose governments they oppose. However, the results of this approach are not always internally consistent. Thus, while members of the British Foreign Office may attend meetings at policy institutes such as Chatham House addressed by Rashid al-Ghannushi, the same Foreign Office officials are not allowed any contact with individuals associated with the Algerian FIS, regardless of their status in Britain.

A harder approach is adopted to those who openly preach violence or dissent, as was apparent in the speech of Douglas Hurd, then British foreign minister, on the occasion of the fiftieth anniversary celebrations of the Arab League in London in 1995. The general tenor of his remarks was to welcome Arabs and Muslims to Britain, but to stress his opposition to those who abused British hospitality in using the U.K. as a base for political activism, whether religiously-inspired or not. His successor, Malcolm Rifkind, has continued to underline the importance of the contributions of Islam to European culture and civilization, as in his opening speech at the EU's Euro-Mediterranean conference at Barcelona in November 1995. The inference remains that political Islam is different from Islam itself, even if that begs questions in turn about the kind of Islamism which can be tolerated in Europe.

As far as joint European initiatives are concerned, the traditional security institutions of NATO (which, of course, is not strictly European) and the WEU have embarked on a series of low-key, bilateral meetings in Brussels with ambassadors from North African and Middle Eastern states. Unfortunately for NATO secretariat staff, the launch of the initial dialogue in February 1995 was somewhat marred by Willy Claes's comments concerning Islamism referred to above. From October 1995, however, meetings with representatives from Morocco, Egypt, Mauritania, Tunisia and Israel have been expanded to include Jordan (although not yet Algeria), with a view to explaining NATO's role in the Mediterranean region in particular and coordinating approaches towards the control of terrorism.

This came at the end of a year which saw the creation of the WEU's joint land and maritime call-up forces, EUROFOR and EUROMARFOR drawn from Portugal, Spain, France and Italy. The role of these forces has been taken to be one of strengthening the articulation of southern European security interests in the Mediterranean,[4] but with what objectives in mind has not yet been made very clear. Vague allusions are occasionally made to the use of rapid deployment forces to intervene in trouble spots in North Africa. However, beyond rescuing European or American nationals still in Algeria, for example, the role of the military in these spheres has not been developed very far. This is partly on account of the political and diplomatic questions still to be resolved in respect of international involvement in the former Yugoslavia, and partly because of the greater interest of France in the evolution of events in Algeria. It is the latter above all which has made any consideration of multilateral international action in Algeria extremely unlikely.

The Algerian situation has also not made the elaboration of European policy towards Islamist activism any easier. Instead of concentrating on Islamism per se, the EU's renovated Mediterranean policy, launched at the November 1995 Barcelona conference, has sought to address the problems of the Mediterranean region in a more global fashion than hitherto. Underlying this Euro-Mediterranean Partnership initiative has been the premise that the region's main sources of tension and conflict (including Islamism) derive from economic instability, and that it will be through strengthening economic cooperation across the Mediterranean basin that future crises will be allayed. The initiative, which includes twelve partners in the Mediterranean region,[5] has as its main goal the creation of a Mediterranean free trade area by the year 2010, to which end a number of new association agreements between the EU and individual Mediterranean partners are in the process of being concluded.[6]

The Barcelona initiative also includes a chapter on the establishment of a political and security partnership—or "common area of peace and stability" in the Mediterranean.[7] Rather than identifying Islamism as one of the causes of instability in the region, however, it is the associated problems of the control of illegal migration, of organized crime, drugs, weapons of mass destruction and terrorism which are detailed as areas for cooperation. There are also provisions for the protection of human rights which generally reiterate undertakings already made by most signatories elsewhere (under the UN Charter, for example), as well as for the promotion of democracy. These provisions are also somewhat vague, since while they stipulate the need for diversity and pluralism in society, they also recognize the right of each signatory "to choose and freely develop their own political, socio-cultural, economic and judicial system."[8]

The avoidance of any direct mention of Islam or Islamism in the EU's policy does not denote any lessening in the preoccupation of European governments with its security implications. Rather, it reflects the lack of a clear European consensus over the extent to which Islamism is a symptom, as much as a cause, of instability in a region so close to Europe's southern shores. By focusing on the clear economic divisions between Europe and North Africa, the EU has been able to forge a broad consensus which would have been impossible to achieve over the more complex issues associated with Islamism. European governments recognize, both explicitly and implicitly, that these issues cannot be swiftly unravelled for the purposes of clearer policy statements.

It is nevertheless the case that the political causes of instability and popular discontent in the Mediterranean have not been addressed with the same thoroughness or attention to detail as their economic roots. In the follow-up to Barcelona, the EU's political dialogue with its Mediterranean partners has been the least developed, and looks set to make only the most general of connections with the social and political grievances which have provided as much popular support for Islamist movements as economic deprivations. In the long run, this does not bode well for the success of European policy in this sphere. However, like much in the still-imperfect sphere of European policy-making, the incentives and motivations of individual European governments will remain subject to the complex perceptions and articulation of national interest. To this extent, a coherent European policy towards Islamism is the last outcome than can be expected, not least because for the purposes of the articulation of both national and European interests, Islamism itself defies any coherent definition.

NOTES

1. *The Unseen Treaty: Treaty on European Union, Maastricht 1992* (3d ed.; London: Nelson & Pollard Publishing, 1995), 34.
2. This is a reference to U.S. Assistant Secretary of State for European Affairs Richard Holbrooke's widely reported comment in February 1996, at the time of the Turko-Greek confrontation in the Aegean Sea, that " while President Clinton was on the phone with Athens and Ankara, the Europeans were literally sleeping through the night."
3. See note 1 above and the discussion by Trevor Taylor, "Britain and Europe's Common Foreign and Security Policy," in *About Turn, Forward March with Europe: New Directions for Defence and Security Policy*, ed. Jane M.O. Sharp (London: Institute for Public Policy Research/Rivers Oram Press, 1996), 92-93.
4. See, for example, Ronald D. Asnus, F. Stephen Larrabee and Ian O. Lesser, "Mediterranean Security: New Challenges, New Tasks," *NATO Review*, no. 3 (May 1996): 28.
5. These are Mauritania, Morocco, Algeria, Tunisia, Malta, Cyprus, Egypt, Jordan, Israel, Syria, Lebanon and the Palestinian Authority.
6. To date, these include agreements with Tunisia, Morocco and Israel.
7. European Commission DG 1B-External Relations, *Euro-Mediterranean Partnership: Barcelona Declaration & Work Programme* (Publication of the official documents of the Euro-Mediterranean Conference, Barcelona, 27-28 November 1995), 2.
8. Ibid.

Islamism Seen from Washington

Robert Satloff

The first question one must ask when discussing U.S. policy toward Islamism is "why is it important?" Lest anyone doubt that importance, rest assured that within the foreign policy establishment, Islamism matters. And it matters not just because it is an important challenge for U.S. policy. We have lots of challenges: the future of Russia, NATO expansion, nuclear proliferation, trade, population, environment, the collapse of multi-ethnic states. These are all challenges of great importance. But Islamism is different. It matters because it is the stuff of a great policy debate.

Indeed, at the end of the twentieth century, dealing with Islamism has provoked one of the few remaining intellectual debates on U.S. foreign policy. Over the last quarter-century, there have been three such debates in the United States, and two of them—the Vietnam debate and the cold war debate—are now academic. This is not to say that the lessons of those two debates don't still resonate in American foreign policy. They do. Vietnam affected very much how we approached the use of force in Haiti, Somalia and the Gulf war. And the cold war debate still very much affects our relations with Russia, our enthusiasm for free markets and the emerging challenge from China. But the Islam debate, which I think you can sum up in five words—"How did we lose Iran?"—is still very much alive, because in many ways the answers to the fundamental question about the events of 1979 still haunt us today in our dealings with governments and political movements around the Middle East. Did we lose Iran because we were too tough on the Shah or because we were too easy on the Shah? What about Khomeini? Should we have been nicer to him or nastier to him? If we had engaged Khomeini earlier, would it have made the revolution more benign? Was the revolution inevitable? Was the collapse of the anti-Shah coalition after the revolution inevitable? Was the anti-Americanism of the revolution itself inevitable and intrinsic to the revolution?

Robert Satloff is executive director of the Washington Institute for Near East Policy.

My purpose today is not to answer these questions but to underscore the fact that these issues continue to enervate scholars, divide policy-makers and resonate in discussions of U.S. policy from Algeria to Egypt to Gaza and beyond. That is one reason why it is important.

A second reason that the Islamism debate is important is more personal. Dealing with Islamism, one must point out, is a very dangerous game. Here, I am not just referring to terrorism, although since the World Trade Center bombing the terrorist aspect of Islamism has vividly come home to America. I am referring to the bureaucratic danger of dealing with the Islamism issue.

Like the cold war debate and Vietnam debate, the Islamism debate within the bureaucracy has a human side with human victims and human casualties. It has hobbled presidents, enfeebled administrations and destroyed careers. The legacy of three episodes—the Iranian revolution and hostage crisis of 1979 and 1980, the blowing up of the Marine barracks in Beirut in 1983 and the arms for hostages deal with the Iranian regime in the mid-1980s—runs deep. I will give you a hypothetical example. Forget about the merits or demerits of the argument about whether there are any moderates in Iran, and simply try to put yourself in the shoes of that assistant secretary of state or that national security council staff director who has reached the intellectual conclusion, for whatever reason, that now is the time to reach out to moderates in Iran. Try to imagine yourself in his (or her) place when he attempts to convince his boss to open a dialogue with the Iranians, which is of course officially sanctioned U.S. policy. What courage he would need! He would not only have to be a very brave bureaucrat, but he would also have to have a wealthy spouse, a nice inheritance, and another line of work to go to when, as he must consider to be a distinct possibility, his career comes crashing to an end when some newspaper in Beirut spills the beans about his contacts or, no less likely, he is simply wrong and the Iranians prove themselves to be not so moderate after all.

It is important to mention these points at the outset because, when all is said and done about the Islamism debate, these two factors—the depth of the intellectual debate and the bureaucratic burden that exists—set the "real world" context in which policy-making is undertaken. Now, let's look at the policy itself.

Lines of a Policy

In my view, the de facto policy of the United States toward the various challenges posed by Islamism since the Iranian revolution has improved over time and is now reasonably coherent and reasonably beneficial to U.S. interests. Namely, we have more or less avoided doing things inimical to our interests, generally restraining ourselves from assisting Islamist movements in their efforts to overthrow friendly and not-so-friendly regimes. This reflects the preeminent rule of policymaking: do no harm. We have even done some positive things in support of local governments engaged in their own face-off with Islamists. And, perhaps most surprisingly, we have even taken some steps of our own—often belatedly, maybe halfheartedly—which have been useful in limiting the spread of Islamism and have perhaps even promoted some semblance of liberalism—one shudders to use the word democracy—in the Middle East. There are exceptions to each of these and I will get to some of them below. But generally our de facto policy has been positive.

More importantly, our policy has been effective. One can have a good policy, of course, that is not effective. U.S. policy has been effective in the sense that only one country—Sudan—has succumbed to the allure of Islamist rule in the past eighteen years. That is really the bottom line. Nothing succeeds like success, and the goal of American policy over the last eighteen years has been to ensure that—for whatever reason we lost Iran—it didn't happen again. And except for the relatively marginal case of Sudan, it didn't happen again.

That is the good news. The bad news, I am afraid to say, is that our policy has succeeded despite an analytical framework that is flawed, overly simplistic and at times curiously counter-productive. This has evolved over time, but when viewed cumulatively, the statements, declarations and public pronouncements of U.S. policy that constitute the official U.S. analysis of the Islamist phenomenon and the formal prescription for dealing with it can only lead one to wonder how it is that there aren't actually more Islamist governments everywhere from Marrakesh to Muscat. Essentially, the actions of the U.S. government are *realpolitik* and the rhetoric is romantic. This gap reflects the role of a certain hesitance, reluctance, and even "political correctness" within the government, as well as the impact of the academic debate on government policy-making.

To illustrate this point, I shall focus on a small number of seminal texts: 1) Assistant Secretary of State Edward P. Djerejian's Meridian House speech of June 1992, the first official statement on U.S. policy towards Islamism; 2) National Security Advisor Anthony Lake's speech and article on the subject of "backlash states," from spring 1994; 3) a very different speech delivered on the same topic at almost exactly the same time (May 1994) by the current Assistant Secretary of State, Robert Pelletreau; 4) an interview of Pelletreau in *Middle East Quarterly*, summer 1995; and 5) the most recent foray on this subject by Edward Djerejian, now director of the James A. Baker III Institute for Public Policy at Rice University, which provides a somewhat different take on the Islamist issue than his 1992 speech.[1] There are other notable statements in the public record, especially President Clinton's November 1994 address to the Jordanian parliament following the signing of the Jordan-Israel Peace Treaty. But because this is a conference presentation, not a dissertation, let me just focus on these key statements and, even more narrowly, on select issues that arise from an analysis of these statements.

To set the framework of this discussion, one must first ask a basic question about U.S. policy: what is the objective? Is U.S. policy inherently reactive about dealing with Islamism, or inherently proactive about advancing certain U.S. interests? The two are very different. For example, one need only examine the titles of the speeches under review. Djerejian's first speech was titled "The United States, Islam and the Middle East in a Changing World"; the Pelletreau speech was titled "Islam and United States Policy"; and the last Djerejian paper was titled "United States Policy Toward Islam and the Arc of Crisis." That 1995 Djerejian paper opened with this fascinating sentence: "A coherent policy framework toward Islam has become a compelling need as foreign policy challenges erupt, involving an arc of crisis." Later, he asked, "What should United States policy be toward Islam?"

These are truly remarkable statements. Policy toward Islam—why? Does the United States have a policy toward Judaism, Christianity or Buddhism? While it is certainly appropriate for the First Lady to host Jewish kids at Chanukkah, Christian kids for an Easter egg toss, and Muslim kids for *knafi* at Eid al-Fitr, articulating a formal policy toward religions is something entirely different. Even suggesting that the United States should have a policy toward Islam, per se, is a major mistake and a fundamental flaw in our approach to the complex issues that are the subject of this conference. The United States has policies towards states, towards institutions (e.g., the United Nations), toward principles (like democracy and human rights), but not toward individual religions. Even to frame the issue in that way is a mistake because it is seen by Islamists as a form of intellectual surrender, with the United States already ceding the ideological high ground to those who want to wage a battle over interests within a religious framework.

In all the documents under review, there is a citation from Pelletreau's *Middle East Quarterly* interview that aptly sums up the best way to approach the issue. "We approach Islamic fundamentalism in a variety of contexts. How it impacts on issues of importance to the United States, such as the peace process. Combatting terrorism, or encouraging open markets, or respect for human rights. The starting point is our objectives, not political Islam as such." Pelletreau was right: defining policy for a global superpower begins with our own interests.

Pelletreau's statement, however, was exceptional. Almost all declaratory statements about U.S. policy are reactive, beginning with political Islam and the various challenges it may or may not pose and only as an afterthought discussing U.S. interests. Given that framework, let us look specifically at three thematic issues—what defines extremism within the Islamist phenomenon, the relationship between economics and extremism, and the question of an "Islamist internationale"—and then two geographic issues—Iran and Algeria—within the overall U.S. declaratory approach to the Islamism.

Extremism and Islamism. Looking over the statements of senior policymakers, there has been substantial evolution in their definition of Islamism and, especially, in their characterization of the extremist element within it. In 1992, Djerejian offered this early definition: "We see groups or movements seeking to reform their society in keeping with Islamic ideals. There is considerable diversity in how these ideals are expressed. What we see are believers in different countries placing renewed emphasis on Islamic principles." In retrospect, this was a fairly rudimentary attempt to characterize different aspects of the Islamist phenomenon. Later in his speech, Djerejian did refer specifically to "extremism," but only in terms of terrorism. That is, extremism within the Islamist phenomenon was limited to specific acts, not to ideas or objectives.

In 1994, Lake took a different approach. "What distinguishes Islamic extremism from other forms of extremism is not terrorism," he said, it is "[t]he naked pursuit of political power." This important statement is the first to equate extremism not with an act but with an objective. Sadly, however, it is also the only statement in all the speeches and interviews under review to make that point.

Pelletreau's statements return to the extremism-as-an-act construction. Indeed, at one point, Pelletreau offered a novel—and highly problematic and potentially dangerous—proposition when he defined extremism in a legal context. "Groups or individuals who operate outside the law," he said in May 1994, "are properly called extremists." That formulation was a step in the wrong direction. Groups or individuals who operate outside the law are more accurately described as criminals in that jurisdiction. Extremists, however, should not be judged so by the legality of their actions. Legality, after all, is a relative term. A simple example will suffice: Hizbullah operates quite legally in Lebanon. Does that make Hizbullah any less of an extremist organization? Of course not. Clearly, legality is not a useful framework for understanding the nature of Islamic extremism. More generally, this spectrum of statements highlights the inconsistency in the approach adopted by U.S. declaratory policy toward the general issue of defining extremism: i.e., is it most usefully characterized by actions or objectives?

Economic Determinism and Islamism. A subset of this issue is the role of economics in the Islamist phenomenon. This is a chicken-and-egg question: what comes first, economic deprivation or Islamic extremism? Which feeds on which? Here, one sees the exact inverse of what one might expect. Since Lake suggested that there is a political basis to extremism—i.e., arguing that extremism is characterized by an objective, not an act—one might logically expect him also to suggest that ideology is dominant, with economics playing only an incidental role in the Islamist phenomenon. In fact, Lake says the opposite: that extremism flows from disillusionment or failure to secure basic needs—i.e., that politics flows from economics.[2] Interestingly, both Djerejian and Pelletreau say just the opposite. Namely, their argument is that extremists find their constituency among those who are economically deprived, but that the extremists themselves exist whether or not there is economic deprivation.[3] Here again is another point of internal inconsistency within the declaratory policy toward Islamism and Islamic extremism.

An Islamist Internationale? Another key issue in this larger debate concerns the international aspect of the Islamic phenomenon, or more specifically, the question of international linkages among Islamist groups and movements. In Washington's view, is there an "Islamist internationale," a "Khomeinintern"? Generally, the official answer is "no." However, looking over U.S. declaratory policy, one can discern a subtle but significant evolution in the U.S. assessment of this issue.

In a famous line from his 1992 speech, Djerejian declared: "We detect no monolithic international effort behind these movements." Two years later, Pelletreau's formulation was slightly different: "We see no monolithic international control being exercised over the various Islamic movements," he said. Given that these were formal statements, not off-the-cuff responses in a question-and-answer session, one must give due weight to this shift in wording. The 1994 formulation appears to imply that there may very well have been an effort to exercise control over various Islamic movements but that it was not successful. More specifically, the statement implies that coordination exists among the movements but not *control*. That shift could have important ramifications.

Radical vs. Moderate Islamism and the Question of Dialogue. The last item to examine is perhaps the key issue for policymakers dealing with Islamism: the analytical debate over the definition of Islamist moderates and Islamist radicals. To what extent does U.S. policy recognize that what separates the two is not a strategic disagreement over goals—they both share the objective of creating an Islamic state founded on Islamic law—but only a tactical disagreement over the appropriate means to achieve that goal, revolution versus evolution? On this issue, U.S. declaratory policy simply punts. Among the various speeches and statements under review, there is no analytical attempt to highlight the "ends versus means" and its connection to moderate versus radical Islamists.

This is not merely an esoteric, intellectual issue—it has operational impact on issues ranging from choosing which Islamists merit "dialogue" with U.S. officials to deciding what sort of electoral systems to recommend to Muslim-majority allies. As Pelletreau said in his *Middle East Quarterly* interview: "I have trouble defining where one category starts and another stops. For example, where in the spectrum do we place the Saudis?" Now, I agree that it may be difficult to place the Saudis at the right point along the Islamist continuum, but policymakers have to make those decisions because they have operational implications. The issue of "dialogue" is particularly important because of the legitimacy and credibility that "dialogue" implicitly endows. Pelletreau answered this question: "Our starting point in the decision of whether to have a dialogue with a group is our total opposition to terrorism and those who practice it. Beyond that, it is *ad hoc*. We examine local conditions, the history of the particular group or movement, and, most importantly, how specific U.S. policy interests would be affected."

I happen to agree with Pelletreau's last sentence because it reinforces the most important aspect of any policy debate—how U.S. policy interests would be affected. But in all the documents under review, that is the only instance where U.S. interests are cited as a key criterion in determining who merits dialogue.

In sum, one can state that a review of these five statements highlights great inconsistency and serious lacunae in U.S. declaratory policy toward Islamism. Of course, it is important to recognize that consistency is overrated—for individuals, it is the hobgoblin of small minds; for states, it is hobgoblin of lesser powers. As a global superpower, the United States has the right (and often the responsibility) to be inconsistent in how it approaches issues such as Islamism, which is why, in the end, our policy has turned out to be quite effective. But if one is looking for intellectual coherence, one will not find it here.

U.S. Policy: What's Missing?

Before I turn briefly to two geographic case-studies, let me take a moment to underscore four themes that are significant *by their absence* from the U.S. analytical discussion of Islamism. For me, these gaps are the most troublesome aspect of U.S. declaratory policy.

First, there is virtually no sense of the true numerical proportion of Islamists. Rarely—if ever—has a senior official noted that Islamists—i.e., Muslims who want to establish an Islamist state—only constitute a minuscule proportion of the more than one billion Muslims in the world.

Rarely—if ever—will a senior official note that Islamist parties have never won a majority in a free election in the Muslim world, that they rarely win more than 30 percent of the vote, and that secularist parties almost always trounce Islamist parties. Instead, U.S. policy statements are riddled with miscues, like the definition of Turkey as an Islamic state in Lake's speech. To most people, Islamic is a normative term, not a descriptive term. As such, Turkey is a Muslim-majority state; Iran is an Islamic state.

Second, U.S. policy statements rarely highlight the real diversity that exists within the Muslim world itself, among Muslims in general, let alone among Islamists themselves. There are virtually no references to the fact that there are hundreds of millions of Muslims who oppose all aspects of the Islamist resurgence, that there are secular Muslims, Muslim social democrats, Muslim free-market liberals or even Muslim communists. Reading the speeches and statements of senior government officials, one would think that there are only two types of Muslims in the world: on the one hand, Muslim who pray five times a day, fast during Ramadan, wear the *hijab* and want an Islamist state; and on the other hand, Muslims who pray five times a day, fast during Ramadan, wear the *hijab*, and don't want an Islamist state. In reality, the vast majority of the world's billion Muslims fits in some other category.

Third, U.S. policy statements are noteworthy for the near-complete absence of discussion about Islamist political goals. Nary a word is said about the fact that Islamists of all political stripes seek the establishment of an Islamic state, with differences among them only about the means to achieve it. (This would be analogous to communists who differ only over whether they seek to replace a liberal-capitalist state through bullets or ballots.) For some reason, U.S. policymakers frequently talk about Islamist "reform" or Islamist "traditional values"—these are American political terms which mean something very different in the Islamist lexicon. For Islamists, reform is not a goal; it is a way station along the road to an Islamist state.

Fourth, and most disappointing of all, is that one rarely hears in American official statements on Islamism any discussion of the role of the state. Analytically, the critical variable in every case-study of the Islamist political challenge has not been the strength of the Islamist movement itself but rather the strength of the state. In Algeria, for example, it took a pitifully small number of tanks to repel hundreds of thousands of protesters, and after all was said and done, a regime whose epitaph was chiseled into granite four years ago is still very much alive. Another well-known example is Syria, whose brutal repression of the Islamist movement in 1982 is certainly not the preferred solution to a political challenge but clearly an option available to states when they believe their very survival is in danger. Here, we should not fool ourselves. After looking at what happened in Iran under the Shah, regimes throughout the Middle East have decided that they will do whatever is necessary to maintain power. The independent variable, therefore, is the staying power of the state; Islamist movements will fill vacuums left by a receding state, but they themselves cannot overthrow the state. An emphasis on the state as the key issue in the Islamist challenge is virtually absent from U.S. declaratory policy on Islamism.

Iran and Algeria

At this point, let us turn to two brief comments on specific cases—Iran and Algeria—where declaratory policy has mattered, in the sense that errors in declaratory policy have worked against U.S. interests. Here, the two poles of the Islamist phenomenon have brought forth statements from government officials that suggest, on the one hand, that Iran is evidence of the permanence of the Islamic revolution and, on the other hand, that Algeria proves the inevitability of the Islamist revolution.

On Iran, I take as my text Anthony Lake's *Foreign Affairs* article, "Confronting Backlash States": "The American quarrel with Iran should not be construed as a clash of civilizations or opposition to Iran as a theocratic state," he wrote. "Washington does not take issue with the Islamic dimension of the Islamic republic of Iran. America has a deep respect for the religion and culture of Islam."

This passage, I believe, was a grievous error. There are certain principles for which the United States stands: democracy, rule of law, government by the consent of the governed, and more. At times, it may be wise to lower the decibel level of our support for these principles, as we sometimes do in dealing with Saudi Arabia, for example. Sometimes, it is wise to be silent. But the United States need never surrender its principles and accord positive legitimacy to a regime whose ideology is opposed to everything that ours stands for, an ideology that mocks America and labels the values we hold dear as "satanic."

Endorsing the "Islamic dimension of the Islamic republic of Iran" was a significant ideological victory for the ayatollahs and a signal of retreat by the United States, although that was surely not the intent of the messenger. In ideological terms, it is precisely the "Islamic dimension of the Islamic republic" that the United States—along with hundreds of millions of Muslims around the world—does oppose, including the Islamic republic's infringement upon the rights of Iran's female citizenry, its religious and ethnic minorities, and others. Legitimacy should not be accorded to any particular form of Islamic rule—it is not only an insult to millions of Muslims but it sends precisely the wrong message about those liberal principles the United States supports and those that Djerejian specifically defended just two years earlier. Of course, for sound strategic reasons, the United States may choose not to accentuate the extent to which we differ with Iran on these issues and we may choose not to base our relations with Iran on their need to modify the "Islamic" dimension of their regime. However, that is a far cry from openly endorsing an ideology that flies in the face of a policy of "democratic enlargement." (Thankfully, this effort at ideological outreach to the Islamic regime—another example of which was a statement by Pelletreau recognizing the "permanence" of the Islamic regime—is no longer a feature of U.S. declaratory policy. Moreover, the laudable efforts at tightening containment of Iran in 1995-96 underscore the Clinton administration's de facto policy toward Iran.)

On Algeria, I take as my text Pelletreau's May 1994 speech: "We agree with the major Algerian parties which insist that the process of political dialogue must involve a broadening of political participation to encompass all political forces in the country, including Islamist leaders who reject terrorism."

To me, this was also a mistake in our declaratory policy. Why, after all, should the United States care whether Islamists are or are not permitted access to the political process? In ideological terms, the United States has standing to advocate on behalf of democrats or liberals—but Islamists? And in strategic terms, the only test of political legitimacy that Washington should justly apply to the Algerian government is whether the Algerian people support the government's political reform program by participating in elections. Apart from general concern over the legality and propriety of an election, the United States should be largely disinterested in litmus tests based on individuals or particular parties. Of course, the Algerians sometimes take advice and often don't. Generally, they know much better than policymakers in Washington, Paris or elsewhere the dynamics of their own society and they did indeed gauge correctly the mood of their people in the November 1995 presidential election, when about 70 percent of the electorate voted for secularist candidates. Since then, the Algerian crisis has moved into a new, more positive phase, both in terms of the domestic political situation inside Algeria and the U.S. approach to it.

Watch What We Do, Not What We Say

If one were to view U.S. policy solely through the lens of declaratory statements, one would fear for the security of U.S. interests in the Muslim world. In fact, as noted at the outset, despite analytical gaps and contradictions, U.S. policy toward Islamism—as implemented, if not as declared—is fairly sound. Specifically:

- The United States recognizes that Islamism poses a distinct threat to U.S. interests and the interests of our allies.

- The United States recognizes that this threat emanates from two sources: sovereign states (e.g., Iran, Sudan) and political movements (e.g., Hamas, Hizbullah).

- Regarding the states, the U.S. has devised a strategy of containment whose objectives range from retribution to resource denial to behavioral change. While containment does not target regime change, per se, if that were a consequence of U.S. efforts, few would mourn their passing. Regarding the movements, U.S. strategy emphasizes three themes: a) counter-terrorism and strong police action, including cooperative efforts by an array of states, from Argentina to the Philippines; b) gradual political reform in host countries, focusing principally (and rightly, in my opinion) on the promotion of individual liberties first and elections second, generally leaving operational decisions about the pace and content of reform to our partner governments; and c) significant doses of economic assistance, either through direct transfers or support for third-party efforts, such as those by international financial institutions.

• Advancing the Arab-Israeli peace process is a key element in the overall anti-Islamism effort. Analytically, this is not an easy argument to make. Lake made the most detailed case for this in May 1994: "Through the peace process, a new regional environment will be created—even now it is taking form—in which moderate Islamic [sic] states from Turkey in the north to Saudi Arabia in the south and from Morocco in the west and Pakistan in the east—will constrain the capacity of rogue states and organizations to extend their influence." In linear form, this arguments runs as follows: peace between Israel and the Arabs will give Arab and non-Arab Muslim governments the freedom to counter extremism at home more vigorously; at the same time, peace will free resources that the state can re-direct into development and attract investment that will promote economic growth; that growth will, in turn, decrease the frustration on which Islamism feeds; and once governments are able to meet the economic needs of their people, they will then feel more secure in meeting their political demands as well; meanwhile, those demands will themselves diminish as the economy grows. This sequence is, I think, a bit too neat—many regimes will be loath to meet demands for political participation for their own reasons, unconnected to peace or the impact of economic reform or growth. Nevertheless, in general terms and especially in the long run, the argument is valid—i.e., peace is good for stability, though the immediate repercussions of peace may be destabilizing for some regimes.

This overall strategy toward Islamism has guided U.S. policy throughout much of the Muslim world, with a notable degree of success. As I said at the outset, eighteen years after the fall of the Shah, the fact that only one other Middle Eastern country (i.e., Sudan) has fallen to Islamist rule is not a bad track record. The two places where we have strayed farthest from this strategy—especially in a declaratory sense—have been in Iran and Algeria; in practical terms, it has not meant much and the policy has largely been corrected. Elsewhere, the U.S. has been surprisingly prudent, generally following the advice Judith Miller advocated in *Foreign Affairs* in 1993, to promote liberalism first, elections second.[4] Advancing the central features of liberalism—the rule of law, minority rights, free judiciaries, freedom of speech, etc.—makes sense because, as Djerejian noted in his 1992 speech, "We know they work."

In conclusion, it appears as though the United States has a reasonably sound policy toward Islamism, articulated very poorly—that is, we generally do the right thing, though perhaps for the wrong reasons. Of course, I much prefer this sequence than the other way around.

NOTES

1. The texts appeared in the following sources, respectively: 1) Edward P. Djerejian, "The United States, Islam and the Middle East in a Changing World," speech delivered at the Meridian House, Washington, 2 June 1992, text in *Mideast Mirror*, 4 June 1992; 2) Anthony Lake, "Conceptualizing U.S. Strategy in the Middle East," speech to The Washington Institute's Soref Symposium, 17 May 1994, and "Confronting Backlash States," *Foreign Affairs* 73, no. 2 (March-April 1994): 45-55; 3) Assistant Secretary of State Robert Pelletreau, "Islam and United States Policy," speech delivered to a symposium, "Resurgent Islam in the Middle East," 26 May 1994, edited proceedings published in *Middle East Policy* 3, no. 2 (Fall 1994): 1-21; 4) Interview with Assistant Secretary of State Robert Pelletreau, "Not Every Fundamentalist is a Terrorist," *Middle East Quarterly* 2, no. 3 (September 1995): 69-76; 5) Edward P. Djerejian, "United States Policy Toward Islam and the Arc of Crisis," paper published by the James A. Baker III Institute for Public Policy, December 1995.
2. "Although the circumstances vary, the phenomenon of extremism around the world flows from common sources—disillusionment, a failure to secure basic needs and dashed hopes for political participation and social justice," said Lake in 1994. "Widespread disenchantment breeds an extremism by no means unique to the Middle East or the Muslim world."
3. "In the last analysis," said Djerejian in 1992, "it is social injustice, the lack of economic, educational and political opportunities that gives the extremists their constituency in each country." Pelletreau used virtually the same language two years later: "In the final analysis, it is in large part the lack of economic, educational and political opportunities that gives extremists of any sort their constituency."
4. Judith Miller, "The Challenge of Radical Islam," *Foreign Affairs* 72, no. 2 (Spring 1993): 43-56.

DISCUSSION

Olivier Roy: It seems to me there is a deep contradiction in the American understanding of this problem. There is this idea that Islamism enjoys the political and strategic backing of Iran, which is the main sponsor of Islamic terrorism in the world. But this is an ideological analysis. If we go back to the facts, to review the main terrorist actions—take, for example, the circles around Shaykh Umar Abd al-Rahman—we see networks that were first established in collaboration with the U.S. and Saudi Arabia, largely on Afghan soil. Suspects in other recent attacks, including the bombings of the U.S. barracks in Riyadh and the Egyptian embassy in Islamabad, have the same organizational pedigree. If we look at the well-known figures of the Egyptian Islamic Jihad movement, they were trained in the 1980s by the Americans, the Pakistanis and the Saudis. Even the Palestinian Islamic Jihad, which is funded and supported by Iran, is now headed by Ramadan Abdullah Shallah, who lectured at the University of South Florida until his recent elevation. It would seem that many Islamist leaders move more readily between Brooklyn and Tampa than between their countries and Tehran. I don't claim that Washington is the center of Islamism, but it has provided a forum.

Robert Satloff: Let us set this question in a context. It is very difficult to convince people outside the United States that bureaucratic errors are not conspiracies. Most Egyptians think that Umar Abd al-Rahman was a guest of the United States way before the World Trade Center bombing; that we knew he was coming, and we welcomed him. The fact is, of course, that he was admitted through a bureaucratic error committed in the American consul's office in Khartoum. As for Ramadan Abdullah Shallah, it came as a complete surprise for every senior policy-maker in Washington that the head of the Islamic Jihad had been sitting in Tampa. The news was a bolt from the blue; people in Washington had never heard of him before. There are gaps in intelligence, and perhaps people in intelligence don't speak as often to the people in policy positions as they should. But one thing there isn't: there isn't a conspiracy on the part of the United States to help Islamic groups, as a kind of policy hedge.

This brings me to the Afghan question. There is absolutely no doubt that we are paying the price for something we nurtured in the 1980s. But the reality is that governments tend to abide by a very simple principle: first things first. You worry about today's problems today and tomorrow's problems tomorrow. Only academics have the leisure to worry about tomorrow's problems today. And in the 1980s, getting the Soviets out of Afghanistan was first priority. Was it a mistake? This was the price of evicting the Soviets, and that achievement must be weighed in the balance against the cost we are paying now.

Daniel Brumberg: You argue that the United States should not tell the Algerians what kind of parties they should or should not legalize. But I think we can have a useful debate about whether Algeria is better off allowing some Islamist party to develop, without placing the United States in the position of telling the Algerians what to do. I happen to believe that every democracy has the right to ban certain kinds of political parties. Here we are in Israel, a democracy which does just that. But I think a case can be made that in Algeria, under certain circumstances, there is room for an Islamic party, and that Algeria may be better off legalizing some sort of Islamic party than not.

Robert Satloff: It is one thing to have a private dialogue with the Algerian government on this question. It is quite another for an official at the highest level, in a formal speech, to state that the position of the United States is that the Algerian government must include Islamist political parties. We should insist that the outcome of their process enjoy popular legitimacy. But how they get there is a matter best left to them.

Ibrahim Karawan (International Institute of Strategic Studies, London): Is there any evidence of interest on the part of American policy-makers in the socio-economic settings that produce a conducive atmosphere for the rise of Islamist extremism? I do not believe much in conspiracies, but sometimes I think that the type of economic shock therapy the U.S. administers becomes a great source of support for the Islamists in their challenge to regimes.

Robert Satloff: When all is said and done, the U.S. gives an awful lot of money to the largest Arab country precisely because not to do so, in U.S. opinion, would be to throw a match on a gasoline-soaked pyre. Economic aid to Egypt began as a political buttress to the Camp David accords, but that original rationale no longer drives our economic aid package to Egypt in 1996. It is precisely to forestall a real economic shock.

As for Algeria, the United States has gone to lengths to address not just the structural issues but also the human issues. For example, the U.S. is working to create a housing mortgage industry in Algeria, which now doesn't exist. We are persuading the World Bank and other institutions to create flows of money, so that Algerian home buyers can borrow. I think that we do recognize the problem. Do we do enough? That remains an open question.

Judith Miller *(New York Times)*: Let me ask you to put on your Warren Christopher hat. You are suddenly secretary of state, and you are in a position to devise a standard for measuring and evaluating what constitutes an evolutionary as opposed to a revolutionary, or a moderate as opposed to a radical Islamist party. Could you do that? Would you do that? Or would you chose instead to say that we are going to deal with Islamism on a case-by-case, state-by-state basis, because movements and their circumstances are so different?

Robert Satloff: If I were Warren Christopher, these questions wouldn't occur to me. Warren Christopher's brief is to develop American relationships with states, while defending and advancing American interests. Warren Christopher's questions should be these: in what way can I help this government? Do I strengthen it? In what ways can I help to alleviate its problems?

Within these limits, the United States does have an opportunity to help advance a more liberal agenda in its dealings with certain states. Take Egypt, for example. In 1991, little could be done: there was a massive terrorist challenge in the heart of Cairo. But today, in 1996, the Egyptians have been reasonably successful in dealing with that challenge. This is the moment to advance a liberal agenda. By a liberal agenda, I mean the rule of law, greater accountability, and protection of minority rights.

But my final comment is that American policy-makers must be modest. The battle between Islamists and governments, between secularists and fundamentalists, is being waged in varying ways in every country of the Muslim world. Yet it is something that can only be affected on the margins by U.S. policy. We can tilt the battle in one direction or the other, but only in the rarest of cases can we decide it.

The Human Rights Jihad

Ann Elizabeth Mayer

In the contemporary Middle East, employing the term jihad does not necessarily signal any commitment to apply the doctrines of jihad as adumbrated in Islamic jurisprudence. Instead, jihad is used as a way to confer Islamic legitimacy on a political agenda in a situation of conflict. In calling the current battles over human rights a jihad, I am suggesting that human rights have come to signify legitimacy in much the way an Islamic reference like jihad formerly did. Increasingly, appeals to human rights are injected into conflicts as if both sides had concluded that they had become the ultimate touchstone of legitimacy.

Whereas the Islamic dimensions of contemporary conflicts in the Middle East and their implications for peace tend to be overemphasized, the human rights dimensions seem to be played down. This is a mistake, since the latter have implications for peace that should not be ignored. There is a growing consciousness within the region that human rights is a central problem facing these societies, and a variety of problems are now labelled as human rights issues. Whether it is tyrannical governments, religious and sexual discrimination, arbitrary criminal justice, torture, censorship, restrictions on travel and freedom of association, or other plagues, the critique of such ills is now based on ideas of human rights. Simultaneously, as Muslims organize to demand human rights and as they grow more familiar with what improvements in human rights might offer, governments deficient in legitimacy are being pressured to take the observance of human rights more seriously and are seeking to coopt human rights. This does not mean that many are making major concessions to demands for human rights in practice. But they clearly feel that they have been placed on the defensive. They now scramble to find excuses for policies not in conformity with international human rights, and deploy propagandists to discredit criticisms of their human rights records.

Ann Elizabeth Mayer is associate professor of legal studies at the University of Pennsylvania.

One result of this has been the concoction of government-sponsored Islamic human rights schemes, models that are supposedly more authentically Islamic than anything that international law offers. These entail misrepresentations, for they are actually artificial hybrids blending international law and Islamic terms and concepts, where any distinctive "Islamic" features are simply wielded to dilute the international principles that they incorporate, eviscerating the rights afforded under international law. Their inadequacy is obvious to the real human rights groups in the Middle East, which have consistently used the international standards.

Iran has been one of the leaders in calling for Islamic human rights. Although the regime has not spoken with one voice on rights issues, its spokesmen have often explained their hostility to international law on the grounds that Iran is entitled to use Islamic principles. Thus, for example, Ayatollah Mohammad Yazdi in March 1995 asked:

> The new issue is this: who says that human rights devised by the West should be applied to the whole world? Who has said such a thing? Some nations have their own cultures, some nations have their own religions, you cannot describe as human rights violations the issues which concern their religion and culture. You cannot impose the human rights as you have translated and defined them...Islamic human rights differ from the Declaration of Human Rights. Islam has its own rules and regulations....The punishment ordained by God's law and mentioned in the Qur'an cannot be ignored. Human rights must be Islamic human rights.

Why does Iran insist on Islamic particularism in the domain of rights? Because it knows that the attacks on its human rights violations are eroding its domestic authority and international prestige. In need of a respectable pretext for deviating from the international norms, Iran, like Saudi Arabia, finds that Islam provides the most serviceable rationale.

Muslim societies are currently torn on rights questions. On the one side there are groups working to secure human rights, including courageous NGOs, in which women often play important roles, and intellectuals seeking to disseminate the values of democracy and civil society. These confront governments or Islamic fundamentalist movements hostile to rights.

Human Rights vs. Islamism

Islamic fundamentalism—used here in the narrow sense defined in the University of Chicago Fundamentalism Project—is antithetical to human rights. Its absolutist and intolerant character leaves no room for pluralism or democratic freedoms. Its exclusivist and reactionary qualities mandate regimes of discrimination against women and minorities. Fundamentalists' zeal to reshape society according to what they believe is a divine plan leads them to disregard the niceties of due process and the rule of law. Respect for rights and freedoms is seen as an obstacle to realizing their programs.

Islamic fundamentalism in this narrow sense can threaten peace. The attitudes of its adherents tend to foster conflicts—although not necessarily ones that are international in scope. Encouraging respect for human rights can mitigate some of the conditions that are proving breeding grounds for fundamentalism, thereby serving the cause of peace. Conversely, flagrant disregard for Muslims' aspirations to have human rights and Western double standards on rights create conditions that tend to make Muslims more receptive to the fundamentalist message, as well as aggravating anti-Western resentments.

Islamic fundamentalism has demonstrable popular appeal. Human rights provide an alternate system competing for people's loyalties—admittedly without the immediate visceral appeal that Islamic fundamentalism has, but one that stands on a much sounder footing in the long run. Human rights offer a way of critiquing fundamentalist programs and policies and discrediting fundamentalists' pretensions to be offering something of enduring value to Muslim societies. The human rights project is realistic and pragmatic, addressing the root causes of many of the worst problems afflicting Muslim societies. In contrast, Islamic fundamentalism is utopian—and utopian schemes are bound to disappoint, as Olivier Roy shows in his book, *The Failure of Political Islam*.

Iranians have had the sobering experience of living under an Islamic fundamentalist regime, and familiarity in this instance has bred an abundance of contempt. Iranians now are equipped to assess the capacity of fundamentalism to solve their problems and are deeply disenchanted with fundamentalist promises. In this connection one sees the turnaround of Professor Abdolkarim Sorush, originally one of the prominent ideologues, some might say henchmen, of the Islamic revolution. After disillusioning experiences, he is now a belated convert to human rights and democratic freedoms. Sorush has learned the hard way about the destruction wrought when religious ideology supersedes human rights. He is finding that he is denied the right to raise questions about the undemocratic way that Iran is being governed or whether rule by the *faqih* does actually embody a definitive Islamic ideology. In difficult circumstances, he has nonetheless managed to win a considerable following; clearly many Iranians today hunger for a dissident message like the one he is trying to communicate.

In the spring of 1996, an Iranian colleague offered an account of a meeting between Iran's President Rafsanjani and Mehdi Bazargan, Iran's first prime minister after the revolution and a devout Muslim who had invoked Islamic legitimacy in his role as a dissident under the Shah. According to the story, in this meeting, which was just before Bazargan's death, Bazargan asserted that the common denominator of the Iranian revolution had not been Islam but human rights. That is, with the benefit of hindsight, Bazargan seems to have had a sharpened perception. Although Islamic fundamentalism did become entangled with the revolution, and Islamic vocabulary and Islamic symbols predominated in the early stages, this did not mean that Islam had provided the real impetus for the revolution. The crucial grievances grew out of the widespread violations of human rights under the Shah. It seems that Bazargan was pressing at the end of his long life for an acknowledgement that indignation over the degradation of human rights had propelled Iranians to revolt. If this account is not actually historically accurate, it is nonetheless valuable as a token of a mind-set now common among Iranians and the way they now focus on human rights issues.

The propaganda line followed by groups hostile to the Iranian regime shows that the opposition appreciates that in the current climate, the regime's bad human rights record is its most vulnerable point—as witness the line of the Mojahedin-e Khalq, who follow an ideology that is a witches' brew of Islam and Marxism and who themselves would not be likely to honor human rights if ever they had the chance to govern Iran. Now the Mojahedin are lambasting the regime for its terrible rights record and in recent publications are seeking to portray themselves as members of the human rights vanguard—rather like an auxiliary of Human Rights Watch.

It is not just in Iran that human rights claims have become the weapons of choice in internecine jihads. In Saudi Arabia, where Islamic fundamentalists are besieging a conservative Islamic regime and contesting its Islamic legitimacy, the government's response has been to invest heavily in propaganda to polish its image in the area of human rights. Thus, since 1990 the Saudis have sponsored the so-called Cairo Declaration of Human Rights in Islam, extolling the virtues of this supremely retrograde document, and in 1992 they promulgated their Basic Law, which includes provision for human rights. In their speeches, the regime's spokesmen have been proclaiming Saudi Arabia's Islamic system of human rights to be the best in the world. For the Saudi royals to pretend to be champions of human rights is patently ludicrous but, nonetheless, politically significant.

The monarchy is facing liberals challenging its repression and attacking its undemocratic system and its violations of rights. The regime has also been belabored by, among others, the minority Shiite community, which launched a program of devastating exposés of the regime's human rights violations before being apparently bought off a few years back. More recently, the monarchy has been plagued by the Committee for the Defense of Legitimate Rights, the CDLR, which in 1993 became the first independent human rights organization ever to be founded on Saudi soil. Repression and threats forced its leader, Muhammad al-Mas'ari, to escape to a London exile, from which the Saudi regime has sought to drive him via pressures on the British government.

Lethal combat between the CDLR and the regime continues. One would expect it to be conducted over Islamic legitimacy, but it seems that human rights have become the centerpiece of this jihad and counter-jihad. The CDLR has deliberately tried to associate its campaign against Saudi kingship with the cause of human rights and democracy. Mas'ari and his group are using human rights cynically since they are as opposed to human rights as the regime is—as shown by their commitment to destroy the UN, international law, and all external human rights monitoring, indicating that they would not want to be bothered by human rights issues were they to come to power. Their real sympathies appear to lie in a particularly reactionary fundamentalist Islam with an admixture of Arab nationalism. While inclusion of terminology like "legitimate rights," with the Arabic adjective being suggestive of a connection with the *shari'a*, does inject some Islamic shadings into its program, the CDLR apparently calculates that Islamic vocabulary and symbols are not sufficient to make clear its appeal. Thus, in the list of CDLR objectives, the very first is

> to elucidate and assert the concept of human rights in Islam and eliminate the distortions created by the Saudi regime's erroneous practices and massive violations of human rights.

One might speculate that CDLR is aiming to impress a foreign audience, but much of its human rights propaganda is directed at the Saudi domestic audience via e-mail and faxes. Thus, one witnesses the surreal spectacle of a conservative Islamic regime and an Islamic fundamentalist movement, both profoundly hostile to human rights, selecting human rights as the arena for waging their contest over who should govern Saudi Arabia. By their hypocrisy in this matter, both indicate that they appreciate that grounding their appeals in Islam is insufficient and that human rights are the criterion by which their programs will be judged. Both are obliged to hope that few will notice the gap between their rhetorical professions of concern for human rights and the thrust of their policies.

The Sudan is another example of how human rights is becoming recognized as the true criterion of legitimacy. The protracted civil war in Sudan broke out again over the 1983 adoption of an Islamic fundamentalist ideology by the Numayri regime. After a democratic interlude and the 1989 coup, Islamization has again been pursued with a vengeance; all resistance is being ruthlessly crushed and a record of egregious rights violations is growing long. The Bashir regime is trying hard to hide its repression and its mistreatment of religious and ethnic minorities and the people of the South. It has mounted a human rights charm offensive, inviting Western visitors for guided tours and selected interviews designed to polish its image and also seeking support from people like the itinerant Louis Farrakhan. The parliamentary elections held in March 1996 seem to be part of this endeavor to show that the Sudan abides by democratic principles.

Some measure of the importance that this regime attaches to human rights can be seen in the fury with which it greets charges of human rights abuses. In September 1995, Abd al-Aziz Shiddu, the minister of justice and attorney general, professed offense over UN reports claiming that

Sudan's version of Islamic law entailed human rights violations, complaining that this was an insult to Islam. This came after his denouncing in March 1994 as "satanic" the work of the UN Human Rights Commission rapporteur, castigating him as an enemy of Islam who had perpetrated an intolerable attack on Islam. That is, Shiddu claimed that it was satanic to point out where the regime's Islamic fundamentalist program clashed with human rights, whereas not too long ago, one could find Islamic fundamentalists insisting that human rights were satanic, as these clashed with sacred Islamic values. Shiddu's violent reaction suggests that there has been a shift in political consciousness and that the normative force of human rights is appreciated even by the retrograde fundamentalists in the Sudanese government. That is, we see a regime noted for its Islamic militancy and engaged in pursuing policies totally at odds with the premises of human rights, acting as though criticism of its human rights record was intolerable and as if no amount of appeals to Islam could suffice to wipe away the blemishes that these criticisms left.

Tunisian Oppression

The clashes between fundamentalist movements and their enemies in secular governments can also be lethal. This is exemplified by the counter-jihad that Tunisia has been waging under President Ben Ali against Islamic fundamentalists. Here, too, human rights figure prominently in the contest, with the Nahda movement focusing its propaganda on Ben Ali's rights violations while pressing the idea that it offers a liberal Islam that can accommodate human rights. Meanwhile, the Tunisian government has undertaken great efforts to associate itself with defending the cause of human rights, investing heavily in cosmetic measures to enhance its image.

In its counter-jihad against the local Islamic fundamentalist movement, Ben Ali's security forces have cast their nets very widely, arresting, imprisoning, and torturing not only active fundamentalists but potentially anyone with the remotest connection to their cause, arresting and harassing family members and not infrequently resorting to sexual assaults on female relatives of suspects and detainees. The fundamentalist opposition has been ruthlessly suppressed, and whatever danger it posed has been eliminated for the present. However, the regime continues to pursue a campaign of repression designed to terrorize all Tunisians into meek submission to rule by Ben Ali, who is, not coincidentally, a former security forces chief. His clampdown goes well beyond the scope of what would be needed to forestall any takeover by Al-Nahda, although the repression is conducted in the name of countering Islamic militancy. Increasingly, it seems that Ben Ali is trying to engineer a situation where the West will have nothing to choose between but his regime and the dreaded fundamentalists. To accomplish this, he is artificially creating a bipolar political situation, which is accomplished by "disappearing" the center of the political spectrum. As has been well described in Ahmad Manai's disturbing book *Supplice Tunisien: Le jardin secret du général Ben Ali*, the security apparatus is going after moderates and liberal democrats, seeking to terrorize the center in order to force its adherents to withdraw as players in the political drama.

The outrageous conviction of Muhammad Muadda in February 1996 (in a trial closed to the press) to eleven years in prison and a fine of $130,000—ostensibly for espionage and collaboration with Libya—shows the kind of war that Ben Ali is waging against political moderates. Muadda was the main opposition leader, the head of a legal party, the MDS (Mouvement des Démocrates Socialistes). He apparently fell afoul of Ben Ali by engaging in open criticism of the ruling party in September 1995. His conviction on trumped-up charges is a serious blow in terms of the setback it means for the chances of constructing the moderate center that could enhance Tunisia's long term stability.

In similar fashion, a friend of mine, Muhammad Najib Husni, has been convicted of a crime that I and others among his friends and colleagues are convinced he never could have committed. Najib Husni is an internationally recognized human rights attorney who, with full awareness of the risks involved, committed himself to defending fundamentalists and political dissidents, distinguishing himself by his dogged defense of the rule of law. His reward for his distinguished services to the cause of justice in Tunisia has been incarceration without trial for about eighteen months, during which he was reportedly tortured, and a conviction for forgery in January 1996 after highly dubious proceedings. The case against him in the estimation of human rights organizations bears the earmarks of being engineered by the government to discredit him and to intimidate other members of the legal profession who might consider trying to defend accused persons whom the regime wants to put away.

Ben Ali is concerned to keep his human rights record looking as good as possible, and he realizes that having political prisoners would make a bad impression. Thus, there are no political prisoners in Tunisia, because the regime goes to great pains to concoct evidence that can be used to convict political dissidents and their associates of crimes other than the acts that actually prompted their prosecution and imprisonment. In consequence, Tunisia officially does not have any political prisoners—only ordinary criminals. Although the results are deplorable—honorable dissidents being denied the dignity of being prisoners of conscience and being treated as if they had committed criminal offenses like spying or forgery—the regime's taking the trouble to set things up this way shows how sophisticated its approach to human rights has become. Lamentably, the West seems to have condoned these efforts at cover-up.

One wonders if some in the West are impressed by Ben Ali's persecution and incarceration of Hama Hammami, the leader of the small communist party and one of the most articulate and outspoken critics of Islamic fundamentalism. One could understand why the West would welcome such a step two decades ago, but today's circumstances are vastly different, prompting this question: How does Ben Ali's locking up a leftist secularist politician serve Western interests? It seems noteworthy that the more open Moroccan system allows secular forces the leeway that they need in order to mount their own campaigns against Islamic fundamentalists.

As the grip of Ben Ali's police state becomes an ever tightening stranglehold on Tunisian society, King Hassan II continues to allow Moroccans to experience incremental expansions in human rights. This is because King Hassan, being politically astute and realistic, appreciates that the pressures for observing human rights are mounting to the extent that the prospects for his dynasty surviving will ultimately be enhanced by accommodating these. Tunisia in early 1996 barred the importation of Moroccan newspapers after they became critical of Tunisia's human rights situation, because Ben Ali could not tolerate having in circulation critical appraisals of his rights record in newspapers from another Arab Muslim country. No one in Tunisia should know that in Morocco's more democratic system, everyone sees through Ben Ali's professions to be championing the cause of human rights.

Clamping down on all and sundry in the manner of Ben Ali is a short-term strategy—both for Ben Ali and for his friends in the West, which has continued to give him strong backing and praise for his achievements. One appreciates that the West sees Islamic fundamentalism as a dire threat, but, in the long run, are Ben Ali's tactics likely to lead to a desirable outcome? Young men with fundamentalist leanings or connections have been thrown into prison, often for terms of ten years. What will happen when these men are released, without having had chances to obtain educations, embittered and with diminished prospects for any kind of successful life? Will this experience of repression lessen the appeal of fundamentalism and its utopian scenarios portraying Islam as the solution to all the ills of society? Will it reduce the political clout of fundamentalism or other anti-Western ideologies after Ben Ali's policies have led to the systematic dismantling of the center of the political spectrum? Is the real problem, contrary to what Samuel Huntington would want people to imagine, not that the West insensitively presses the universality of human rights, but that the West is turning a blind eye to human rights abuses committed by friendly regimes that claim that recourse to violence and repression are needed to eliminate the Islamic fundamentalist threat?

Another sign of the importance of human rights is that these are now part of the arsenal of weapons used in interstate conflicts between governments of Muslim countries, with charges of human rights violations being hurled in propaganda jihads. For example, a coalition of Kuwait, Iran, Saudi Arabia in 1995 joined other states in the UN in condemning Iraq for its human rights violations. Now, one is entitled to query whether these three states were really aggrieved at Iraq because of its human rights violations, or whether the condemnation was prompted by their shared political animosity to the regime that had invaded the first two and threatened the security of the last. It is interesting that three states, all with such problematic domestic human rights records domestically, should want to go on record as condemning Iraq on the basis of its human rights violations.

Iran, in response to widespread foreign criticisms of its rights violations, seems to feel compelled to take the offensive on rights issues, being irresistibly drawn to arguments grounded in international—not Islamic—human rights, and it tries to exploit their normative power, which it implicitly recognizes. For example, it attacks Saudi Arabia for its failure to adhere to human rights. Thus, Iran's state news agency commented on the November 1995 bomb attack in Saudi Arabia, saying that the crisis was not surprising because "violations of human rights and widespread social and cultural discrimination are commonplace in Saudi Arabia."

Western Double Standards

Iran also complains that U.S. castigations of its rights record are biased, contrasting these with the U.S. tolerance of rights violations by Saudi Arabia. See in this connection the bitter speech by Ayatollah Khamenei on 2 November 1995, complaining that for the U.S. it did not matter whether a government respected human rights or not, whether there was democracy in its country or not. Khamenei claimed:

> If you look at the Middle East, you can see governments which are accepted and approved by the American hegemonists. In terms of their ideology, political development, from the point of view of human rights record, democracy, what type of government are they? Do they understand the meaning of democracy? Do their people understand what an election is? Could anybody assume that there is room to breathe in those countries? Not at all. It does not make any difference to officials of an hegemonic country, such as the U.S. The important thing for the U.S. is that those countries submit to it. That is sufficient.

Khamanei had a point. By acting so inconsistently, by excoriating Iran for human rights abuses while cosying up to Saudi Arabia—with human rights violations at least as bad and with, overall, a more closed and repressive political system—the United States was bringing discredit on Western professions of concern for human rights, conveying the idea that political agendas were central ingredients in human rights policy.

Meanwhile, Mas'ari and his ilk are charging that international law and the UN simply serve the political interests of Western powers. Assuming a world based on the "West-against-the-rest" thesis, they conclude that the entire international system is fatally biased. The CDLR rejects the notion that the U.S. accords high priority to human rights and warns:

> The U.S. unconditional support for the Saudi government will undoubtedly have adverse effects on the interests of the American people, who are hereby called upon to protest against their government's policies. The Saudi people, who are determined to restore their rights and put an end to the injustices practiced against them by the present regime, hold the U.S. government responsible for the continued violation of human rights and for the corruption that is costing Saudi Arabia its wealth and independence. Those who wish to deal with Saudi Arabia are reminded that the entire region is undergoing a comprehensive popular renaissance, and therefore they need to take the popular will into consideration.

It is not just regimes like Iran or zealots like Mas'ari with political axes to grind that are complaining about the double standards that the West uses in the human rights area. In March 1996 Musa Bin Hitam, the outgoing Malaysian chair of the UN Human Rights Commission, slammed the West for condemning human rights abuses in some states while letting political or economic allies "literally get away with murder," asserting:

> The biggest obstacle to achieving understanding in the field of human rights is the political factor that is injected into discussions almost every time it arises at the international fora. We see double standards again and again. The word is out that if you want to abuse human rights, make sure that you are the best of friends of the big powers that matter, then you can get away with it.

When the modern system of human rights was set up, people appreciated that it would be destructive if it were ever seen to have become a tool of power politics. To the extent that it is now associated with great powers protecting and rewarding their friends and using charges of human rights violations to embarrass their enemies, the viability of the entire system is being jeopardized. This politicization is not in the interests of preserving an international system of human rights or of preserving respect for international law generally. If it were only the CDLR that was calling for the destruction of the UN and for Muslim countries to lead the exit from it, it would not be so worrisome. But the disenchantment with double standards in the application of human rights standards is causing a much wider disillusionment. The implications for peace are troubling since the UN, with all its weaknesses and failings, is an important guarantor of peace, a vital forum for resolving differences before they explode in wars.

It is not obvious that the West appreciates how deeply Muslims are concerned with human rights violations afflicting their fellow Muslims and how profoundly embittered they have become by the UN's failure to protect these rights, for which they hold the West to blame. Western hypocrisy and Western policies of indifference to Muslims' human rights can be exploited by fundamentalists to whip up anti-Western sentiment and to promote attitudes inimical to peace. The West already saw this in Iran, where the Shah's dismal human rights record and the unswerving Western support for his rule created an anti-Western backlash, which fundamentalists exploited to mobilize Iranians against the West as the ally of the ruler who created so many Iranian martyrs.

Now, one appreciates that lying and hypocrisy are not about to be banished from the realm of politics and international diplomacy and that the great powers cannot be expected to conduct foreign affairs as if they were agents of Amnesty International. Nonetheless, there is a problem when the disparity between pious moralistic rhetoric about human rights and the actual policies pursued by Western foreign ministries grows too glaring. Especially in the case of conflicts in which Muslims are seen as the victims of non-Muslims' aggression and oppression, the Western failure to intervene to condemn and deter violations of Muslims' rights can severely aggravate anti-Western antagonism and prompt calls for jihads against Western influence.

There are all too many examples of Western indifference in the face of grievous rights abuses afflicting Muslims. Probably the most dramatic contemporary example is Bosnia, where the world stood by in the face of genocide and ethnic cleansing directed against Muslims, systematic mass rapes, incarceration in concentration camps, terror, torture, and the like, and where the worst abuses were mostly carried out by the Christian forces of the Orthodox Serbs and Catholic Croats. The failure to organize measures to forestall the ghastly carnage and cruelties confirms the impression that West does not care about human rights where Muslims are the victims and does not want Christians held accountable for violating Muslims' rights.

The world should have predicted that Bosnians' plight would prompt empathy on the part of other Muslims, that in the wake of the Bosnian horrors, they would be crying for revenge for the wrongs inflicted on their coreligionists. It should have come as no surprise that Iranian and Saudi *mujahidin* were found in Bosnia preparing terrorist attacks on Western and UN forces in February 1996. Nor should one be astonished that in March 1996 there came a report of Bosnians sending soldiers to Iran for training, a natural outcome of the West's unconcern for the sufferings of Bosnia's Muslims. After the protracted Western indifference to war crimes in Bosnia, the Bosnian government has naturally wanted to keep ties with Muslim countries like Iran as a form of insurance, should the West again decide to allow Muslims to be slaughtered, tortured, and raped en masse.

Did the West not set the stage for Bosnian Muslims' estrangement by talking endlessly about human rights and then showing callous disregard for the plight of Bosnia's Muslims? As Margaret Thatcher has appreciated, the Western failure to act in a manner consistent with proclaimed humanitarian ideals and the decision not to intervene to stop the massive violations of human rights of Bosnian Muslims had the potential to engender a BLO, a militant counterpart of the PLO in Europe. Has Margaret Thatcher gone wobbly? It seems more plausible that her stance on this question comes from her being tough-minded and pragmatic— and seeing accurately the danger of discounting the fallout that can come from treating violations of Muslims' human rights casually at a time when Muslims' sensibilities in this area are aroused.

The Centrality of Human Rights

Stereotypes being purveyed by people like Samuel Huntington and simplistic generalizations about supposedly monolithic Western and Islamic civilizations confronting each other and clashing over rights issues cry out for skeptical appraisal. These can distract one from noticing the centrality that debates over human rights policy have assumed within Muslim societies and the significance of the jihads and counter-jihads that are being waged over rights issues. Muslim countries are meanwhile injecting human rights issues into their quarrels with rivals.

Misguided and insensitive Western policies on rights issues affecting Muslims have the potential to exacerbate conflicts and strain the fibers of the international legal system. Muslims have reacted with anger and resentment over Western inconsistency and double standards and Western disregard for human rights violations where Muslims are the victims and non-Muslims the perpetrators. There is reflexivity in the treatment of rights. The West's setting a bad example by backing regimes brutally repressing dissent and mistreating Islamic movements and their supporters can intensify rather than mitigate the appeal of Islamic fundamentalism. Western alliances with regimes that disregard Muslims' aspirations to enjoy human rights may appear to be dictated by tough-minded *realpolitik* but in fact may merely result from shortsighted miscalculations that accord too little weight to human rights concerns. By the way we in the West respond to human rights problems involving Muslims, we are educating a wider public than we may initially realize about whether human rights standards can become the organizing principles for Muslim societies and the international community in the next century.

DISCUSSION

Participant: Is there any modest hope that Islamists may be learning something in the dynamic process of politics that is under way in the Middle East? As the potential beneficiaries or actual beneficiaries of human rights, do they pause to consider that there might be some virtues in this system? Might they be marginally less quick to denounce and deny the instruments they have benefitted from?

Ann Elizabeth Mayer: First, the Islamists are not always the prime beneficiaries. It depends so much on the country. Morocco has a relatively open political system for an Arab country, and the primary beneficiaries in Morocco of democratization are the non-Islamist or non-fundamentalist parties. Similarly, in Tunisia there is a big left and a substantial center, and the impression is that Ben Ali is closing out people who are not fundamentalists in the name of repressing fundamentalists. I don't think we can assume that the Islamic forces in the political scene will necessarily be the primary beneficiaries of greater respect for human rights or democratization.

But the problem, of course, is what kind of lesson the Islamists are learning about human rights and democracy. There are some who really have been profoundly touched by having been deprived of their own human rights, and so have developed a commitment to them. About others, I am very skeptical. I think the CDLR people are cynics who deploy human rights opportunistically. But one can only hope that the more these ideas circulate, the more they will inhibit those coming to power. These ideas could tend to weaken their authority and to delegitimize their regimes if, having preached devotion to these principles on the road to power, they took over and renounced the very principles they had championed.

But there are discouraging precedents. We must remember the lead-up to the Iranian revolution, when so many reassuring noises were made about how Islam would be combined with respect for rights in a way that would preclude the emergence of anything like a totalitarian regime. This reassuring picture was quickly eclipsed by the present clerical regime, which ever since then has been unwilling to allow genuine pluralism.

Ibrahim Karawan (International Institute of Strategic Studies, London): What about the stand of Islamists now in opposition, regarding violations of human rights in populist Islamist regimes? I am thinking of Sudan and Iran in particular. Do considerations of Islamist solidarity lead Islamists to look the other way or even justify rights violations by these populist regimes? And if they don't take a stand regarding violations in Sudan, why should we be impressed by their proclamations that they will adhere to human rights?

Ann Elizabeth Mayer: One case of a falling down on this point in the leader of the Tunisian Islamist opposition, Rashid al-Ghannushi, whom many people regard as a moderate. One reason I have no respect for Ghannushi is that he defends the Sudanese regime. When he talks about his commitment to human rights and democracy, and at the same time absolutely whitewashes what has happened in the Sudan, his credibility goes out the window. This is indeed a real test of whether Islamists are serious about human rights.

Daniel Pipes: You seem to assume that American policy, if not Western policy in general, should be based solely on human rights considerations. Yet we obviously have other interests besides human rights, which can only be one factor among many that set parameters for foreign policy.

In the Middle East specifically, policymakers face a Hobson's choice between the regime and the opposition. In the case of your despised Ben Ali, we have chosen to go with him for lack of certitude that his opponents would be any better. We went with the Shah. We are going more or less with the regime in Algeria. This is not because we are blind to their faults, but because we think they are probably better than the alternatives. This is not so much a generic foreign policy problem, as it is a problem of the Middle East, where the grim choice is between dictators and would-be dictators. We are left to pick the dictators who are most amenable to us.

Ann Elizabeth Mayer: I didn't say that foreign policy should be based solely on human rights. But I am concerned when an insensitivity towards human rights issues leads to a backlash and a tremendous loss for the West in the long term. I think that the example of Iran is well chosen to illustrate this point. In the 1950s, a basically middle-class nationalist movement could have taken power. But the U.S. made a short-term calculation: better for the oil industry not to have Mosaddegh in power, better to have Mosaddegh overthrown and the Shah restored. The West intervened very energetically to restore a very unpopular monarch, and the West sustained him for all those years when his human rights violations made him hated by nearly every segment of Iranian society. The result was the Islamic revolution.

I'm not sure how fair it is to second-guess people with hindsight. But I think everyone who knew Iranians also knew how profoundly detested the Shah had become, and could deduce that his kingship was extremely fragile. I wrote a paper in 1965 saying that he would be gone by 1975. I was off by four years, but it seemed to me clear that he was doomed.

Yes, a trade-off is involved. But it must always be remembered that short-term gain can end in long-term loss. In the short term, backing someone like Ben Ali might make sense; he is undoubtedly a friend of the West. But in the long term, backing Ben Ali could prove disastrous. Qadhdhafi in neighboring Libya, despite his remarkable staying power, could be swept away by an Islamist revolution. Algeria is profoundly unstable. What will happen if these countries go under and we have a really hated dictator in Tunisia? I don't know, but it's a question that deserves asking. When I was in Tunis and talked to people in the American embassy, they didn't seem to recognize that this was a question that needed to be addressed. One might tally all the trade-offs and still legitimately conclude that Ben Ali is the choice. But I'm not sure that anyone is doing any tallying at all.

Robert Satloff: There are different kinds of human rights. There are individual restraints and collective restraints. I have always thought it was more useful from an American perspective to focus on the liberal individual. Which sort of hierarchies are Islamists constructing? Are they on the individual side of the wide spectrum or on the collectivist side? And specifically, how are they talking about the issue of minority rights, which in my view is the litmus test?

Ann Elizabeth Mayer: Islamists always treat the minorities issue very evasively because it is too embarrassing to deal with it in a straightforward way. Look at the Iranian constitution. It speaks of recognized minorities and the protection of their rights as equals—and then goes on to add qualifications that discriminate against non-Muslims. This kind of sleight of hand is very common and very disturbing.

But the denial of minority recognition and rights is not unique to Islamic fundamentalist discourse. A similar sleight of hand is the tendency of the Egyptian government to deny that there is a Coptic minority. I have had some very heated arguments with Egyptians, who insist that there is no difference between a Copt and a Muslim, and that therefore no Coptic minority exists. This kind of denial is taken to an extreme in the most secular state of all, in Turkey, whose inhabitants are all defined by the constitution as Turks. There is no such thing as a recognized minority in Turkey.

As for Islamists, they use various verbal subterfuges that skirt the issue of whether they intend to adhere to human rights as set forth in the international covenants. That poses a problem, because if they are not willing to speak frankly about their stance, dialogue becomes difficult if not impossible.

Is Islamism the Future?

Probably, affirms Graham E. Fuller, but there is no cause for panic, because the responsibilities of power will make Islamists conform. No, replies Martin Kramer: Islamists will fail, unless mistaken policies surrender power to them. In that case, expect the worst.

Islamism(s) in the Next Century

Graham E. Fuller

This essay represents an attempt to look at the future challenges of Islamic movements as they move into the next century: the kinds of problems that will arise for them, the alternatives they possess, and the problems they will raise for others. This examination clearly must be rather theoretical and speculative in nature, but a good bit can be said based on the realities we see in the Muslim world today—differing situations with differing characteristics that help shed light on possible future courses of action for Islamists.

Assumptions

I make a number of assumptions about the future of Islamism in the Muslim world on which my discussion is based.

First, Islamic movements are considerably diverse from state to state. A number of movements have willingly embraced violence: Islamic Jihad (Palestine and Egypt), Hamas (Palestine), FIS (certain elements), Gama'a Islamiyya, and more. Others eschew political violence: Hamas (Algeria), Muslim Brethren (Egypt), Al-Nahda (Tunisia), Refah (Turkey), Jama'at-e Islami (Pakistan), and others. The willingness to employ violence is not merely a function of the political ideology and tactical approach of the group involved, but more importantly, also reflects the political culture of the state involved—especially the degree of state violence or state terror employed.

Second, Islamic movements are evolving. They have witnessed much and learned much since coming into existence—some possessing long years of organizational experience, others much more recently founded. The learning process starts with the tactical requirements of surviving as a political movement or party in the face of a hostile state. It also requires the evolution of new political concepts, derived from both Islamic and

Graham E. Fuller is a senior analyst in the international policy department at RAND.

non-Islamic sources, as they relate to the reality of their political programs. This process of evolution is entirely natural and, more important, necessary. After all, Islamist movements are appearing for the first time in modern history in the context of a modern independent state. Islamist movements are required to deal with complex new political realities, with the state (usually authoritarian), and with a variety of international conditions, involving both other Muslim countries as well as non-Muslim powers further afield.

Third, the conditions themselves under which Islamist movements are evolving are diverse, and exert major impact on the character of the emerging Islamist movements. Many of our criticisms of the character of these Islamist movements are, in fact, simultaneous critiques of the state political cultures involved: how much do state methods shape the Islamist opposition? "Chicken and egg" problems exist here. For example, was it the Egyptian state or the Muslim Brethren which first opened to the door to real political violence? In most cases, the state bears the primary responsibility for introducing the concept of political violence through its own violent repression. Does the non-violent character of the Islamist Refah party in Turkey reflect the virtues of the party itself, or perhaps does it say more about the rather open and democratic political environment in which it operates? On the other hand, Algeria's Hamas party has managed to eschew violence in a highly violent context—but also in a context where the more radical and dominant Islamist movement within the country has already turned to violence, leaving Hamas the option of playing on the margins as a non-violent movement. It can be argued that Al-Nahda in Tunisia has avoided violence despite the practice of state violence against it.

Fourth, the phenomenon of Islamist movements is as integrally linked to local politics as almost any political party in the Muslim world could be. They are more "authentic" and more deeply grounded in the political grass roots than most other parties; they are less elitist, and probably more closely in touch with popular concerns than most other parties. Arab nationalist movements were also able to touch wellsprings among the masses, but were nonetheless usually more elitist in character, with strong representation of the intellectual class, usually ostentatiously lacking support of more bourgeois or business circles, or lower classes. Gamal Abdul Nasser probably came as close as any Arab nationalist to tapping genuine popular wellsprings. Their genuine rooted populism gives the Islamist movements considerable prospect of longer life in the Arab world.

Fifth, the conditions that help bring Islamist (and potentially other opposition movements) to the fore are not likely to go away soon. These conditions are primarily internal, springing from the shortcomings and failure of regimes in power. They can also be external, however, usually where non-Muslim power is seen as oppressive to Muslims (Palestine, Azerbaijan, Bosnia, Kashmir, for example). As long as these conditions persist, there is no reason to believe that they should not continue to lend strength to Islamist movements.

Sixth, these Islamist movements are not likely to be eliminated by force or repression. Conditions will vary from state to state, but state violence usually increases desperation and hence feeds public sympathy and support for the Islamists. There obviously exists, however, some point at which state repression has some effectiveness; at that stage such movements will fail to gain more power as the cost and risks of membership increase. But by and large, violence and repression will be ineffective or counterproductive in preventing the spread of sympathy and support for Islamist movements. The reputation of Islamist movements can mainly only be damaged by their own actions, not the actions of others.

Seventh, there are only three ways in which Islamist movements are likely to begin a broad decline in popularity and support. First would be major success by existing regimes in solving the critical problems of life within the state. As desirable as this is, this eventuality seems rather unlikely in most Muslim states. Few countries are models of policies where consistent progress in being made to the net gain of the regime in power. Possibly, only possibly, might Tunisia, Morocco, Kuwait, Jordan, Malaysia and Indonesia qualify in this capacity.

A second alternative for the decline of Islamism might come through the rise of alternative political movements that tap the same popular wellsprings of support, trading off the same grievances. There seem to be few parties on the horizon that would be able to fulfill this task. Arab neo-nationalism is one prospect for the future, but so far nothing has emerged that has been able to successfully reformulate the old and tired Arab nationalist rhetoric—indeed, the exploited and distorted nationalist message—except perhaps a clear and present threat from a non-Muslim power. Thus Arab nationalism still retains in Palestine a viability rarely seen elsewhere—in direct competition with Islamist forces. Few other regions in the Muslim world present this contrast. Arab nationalism almost certainly will reemerge in new and more enlightened garb in the future, but it is not clear when and under what circumstances. Bourgeois or liberal parties regrettably seem to be out of touch with mass aspirations in most countries at this stage. Military coup would seem to be only remaining alternative to the Islamists in power (or out).

The third potential cause of decline of Islamist movements will come from the patent failure of Islamists in power to bring about substantive change and improvement of the kind sought for by the broad population. Because of the general exclusion of Islamist parties from power, they remain untested, and thus maintain a residual appeal that is hard to counter until tested. Islam in power in Iran and Sudan, for example, will hardly leave a legacy of enthusiasm for more of the Islamist option in the future. Islamism driven to extraordinary violence by the state—Algeria and Egypt—just might frighten broad segments of the public away from them, but not for long if the state persists in patterns of failure and the perception of illegitimacy. Small tastes of Islamist policies in partial power—Turkey, Jordan, Pakistan—may already serve to limit some of the popular appeal of these movements.

These seven assumptions inform the remainder of my discussion.

Sources of Future Islamist Strength

The future of Islamist power obviously rest on the determinants of Islamist strength. What are the main preconditions for the emergence of strong Islamist movements in the Muslim world? Some of these have been noted above. Briefly, the most important preconditions start with the failure of the state and the state order. This means states and regimes dealing ineffectively with economic and social grievances—employment, food, housing, social infrastructure, and social services including health and education. Second, the state is usually vulnerable to charges of illegitimacy in never having met the test of popular support in elections, and to charges of corruption, favoritism, and moral weakness in Islamic terms. Third, political repression and authoritarianism are important preconditions for the emergence of strong Islamist movements. Fourth, implicit in the authoritarian order is the absence of alternative political parties, forces and movements; the state has usually emasculated or eliminated alternative parties so that they enjoy only marginal support in certain narrow segments of society. The Islamists thus become the only viable alternative to regime power. Some regimes actually put the choice just that baldly: Mubarak in Egypt thus tells the public that the only choice is between him and the Islamists. Such tactics may work for a while, but invariably lead to the hollowing out of support for the regime, leaving street power to the Islamists in the end.

Fifth, Islamist regimes flourish when discredited regimes are in close proximity to non-Muslim power. Arafat's PLO has moved towards this danger. Saudi Arabia's legitimacy is under strong challenge due to its close security ties with Washington that are seen primarily to support the regime. Finally, Islamist movements flourish when they are linked with struggles of Muslim peoples for separatism or national liberation. Here again the Palestine situation comes to mind, as does Bosnia, Kashmir, and Uighurs in Xinjiang, among others. Similar situations exist in Kazakstan and some other Central Asian states where the highly compromised character of regime cooperation with Moscow combines with the need to formulate a new national character (a character never forged in the sudden "gift" of unsought independence following the collapse of the Soviet empire). While Islamist movements are only slowly emerging where Islam had been all but destroyed under seventy years of communism, Islam almost surely is in the process of being integrated in the nationalist project by which Kazaks, Kyrgyz and others are seeking to build a new national entity in which not only language, but also Islam helps distinguish them from the Russian "other."

Islamist Options When Out of Power

Islamist parties out of power must chart a course that will preserve their long-term survival, strengthen their ranks and clout, and finally that will eventually bring them to power. The kind of course they choose will reflect to a considerable degree the nature of the political challenge posed to them by state—ranging from ban and repression, to tolerance and opportunities for democratic competition, and so forth. But each party must first decide whether it will focus first on the creation of a foundation for long-term growth of Islamist political sentiment in the country, or on the mechanisms of gaining power. The former strategy, often referred to as *da'wa* or *tabligh* activities (i.e., missionary or propagation), seeks to create the groundwork of Islamist awareness, political consciousness, and political education that will gradually transform the political and social environment in favor of Islamist values.

This choice resembles in part the classic communist debate—Lenin, Trotsky, Stalin, the Mensheviks, etc.—about whether first to create the appropriate preconditions for communism via education, economic preconditions, and institution-building, or simply to seek power first and then use that leverage for the imposition of ideological goals.

The choice is not a black and white one since the two methods are not entirely contradictory. Islamist movements will always seek to gain adherents within key structures of the state in order to facilitate the building of support and cadres. Opponents of the Islamists call this "infiltration"; sympathetic observers would describe it as typical political activity designed to build cadres conducive to gaining influence in the society. Thus the ministry of education might be one key target of the Islamists where they seek to influence the kind of education about Islam that will affect future generations and their outlook. The Jama'at-e Islami in Pakistan strongly emphasized educational activities. Hasan al-Turabi in Sudan placed great emphasis on influencing or controlling the educational agenda in Sudan in the long years before coming to power via coup in 1989—probably assisted by this groundwork. Opponents of the Refah party in Turkey similarly accuse it of infiltrating educational establishments in order to purvey its message and shape the agenda.

Building of cadres in interior ministries can serve to deter or provide early warning to Islamist movements from hostile moves by security services. In a more Leninist vein, again like Turabi, the building of cadres within the armed forces can lay the groundwork for future sympathies within the military—either to support an Islamist coup, or to prevent the military from using force against Islamist movements or demonstrators. This kind of bureaucratic power is exceptionally important because, as in the case of Sudan, it directly facilitated the pro-Islamist coup.

The challenge posed by these Islamist political activities is therefore complex and requires serious examination. All political activity in one sense can be viewed as a process of "infiltration," of establishing adherents and ideological allies in key posts—witness the immense political stakes perceived in the American process of appointing justices to the Supreme Court, or specific individuals to cabinet posts. Islamist interest in affecting national outlook and the ability to craft national policies is entirely familiar in Western politics. The dividing line comes when one talks of tightly centralized parties, the "Leninist" model where all attention is turned to the process of gaining power above all else. The precondition for leveling the charge of "dangerous infiltration" against Islamist political activity in any accurate fashion requires the perception that the party involved indeed is Leninist, intensely disciplined, and able to operate without other "natural" political restraints which would dilute the effectiveness of their goals. Such natural restraints would be size and transparency of the party, existing institutional restraints such as large ministries that cannot be readily taken over, etc. The problem again relates at least as much to the political culture of the individual state than to the Islamist movement itself.

Islamist parties thus face the traditional challenge faced by so many ideological parties about when to assume power. This question differs between a democratic and non-democratic order. In a democratic order the calculus needs to be made as to whether the party will flourish by coming to power under particular circumstances, whether a coalition should be joined or not joined. If the calculations of many observers, including myself, are correct, that Islamist parties will suffer loss of popularity in actually taking responsibilities for policy making—because they probably lack any real answers to the problems which exist—then many Islamist parties may avoid entry into coalitions simply because the role of opposition may be more effective and less demanding than assuming policy responsibilities.

In non-democratic orders, the calculus is entirely different, because all groups are looking for openings by which to attain power and that opening is often available only by coup. Where coups are not feasible, influence can only be attained either by cooperating with the existing regime—as in Jordan or Yemen or Pakistan, all quasi-democratic—or else by assuming a position of outright opposition to it. For most Islamist movements in non-democratic states, the role of opposition, legal or illegal, would seem the most beneficial. It benefits them not to cooperate with regimes perceived as ineffective, corrupt, or illegitimate. And this is why the Islamists are perceived as dangerous to existing non-democratic orders. As in Algeria or Egypt, the state finds it more advantageous to goad the Islamists into violence in order to justify total crackdown on the basis of "struggle against terrorism." In the final analysis, when options for gaining political power emerge, few political movements will turn their back on them simply because the conditions are "not right."

Next, Islamist movements need to develop political and tactical principles in relation to the existing political situation. This requires an operational sensitivity to the political scene. Mere insistence on broad ideological principles may be of little avail if opportunities to benefit from the political and social order are missed. How do Islamist movements mesh their ideals and principles with the practice of politics? Are the two arenas—the realm of power and the realm of principles—entirely insulated one from the other, so that the means of gaining power remain divorced from the ideological task of implementing ideals once power is attained? To gain power by any means first, and then worry about implementation of ideals later? This approach is of course entirely opportunistic, in which the ends and means of the Islamist party (or any other party) are divergent.

The temptation of the totally opportunistic approach to gaining power is particularly inherent in non-democratic orders where the possibilities of otherwise attaining power are almost non-existent. One of the major dangers of authoritarian government is that it eliminates the political arena in which political experience and eventually political maturity might emerge. In other words, the Islamist party, focused on power alone, would never have occasion to learn anything from the political process itself, including compromise, policy experimentation, and the evolution of new principles in the pragmatic exercise of power and administration.

As noted above, almost nothing in this discussion is unique to the problems of Islamist parties but is characteristic of all political parties that must make constant similar choices between purity of ideology, tailoring that ideology to mass appeal, and the requirements of gaining power in order to implement a program. Still, strongly ideological parties run the inherent danger of being more willing to "compromise" ("say or do whatever it takes"), because the ideological message in principle can be kept pure "pure" and subordinated to the requirements of gaining power until power is attained.

A second key area of decision-making for Islamist movements is the use of political violence. This choice is often determined by the state first when it employs violence or terror against Islamist parties, especially in extra-legal manner. Islamist violence can be directed either against the oppressive state itself, or against some external enemy. The decision to use violence is a risky one, but it also can be effective in several circumstances, whether by Islamist or non-Islamist groups. First, Islamist violence against the state invariably focuses on the illegitimacy of the state in Islamist eyes: on regimes that are neither elected, nor able to gain legitimacy by meeting the needs of the people. Where the state bans legitimate political activity of the Islamist movements or parties, it further loses legitimacy in the eyes of the Islamists.

Violence can also draw attention—especially international—to grievances within the state, suggesting that the state is not in control, that it has determined opposition, and that foreign states might wish to rethink the nature of their relationship with the regime in question if it might appear to be shaky or unpopular. Violence by Islamist groups in Algeria, Egypt, Bahrain, and Saudi Arabia, are examples. Violence can also serve to polarize politics within the state, to let the population know that a determined opposition exists and is willing to take on the illegitimate state.

Violence is a far less effective means of political action where the state is otherwise legitimate in the eyes of the public. (Turkey, Jordan, Kuwait, and Morocco might fall into this category, where regimes are seen as somewhat responsive to the people, even if not fully democratic.) Violence pursued by Islamist parties in this context delegitimizes the party itself. Thus the question of Islamist violence is largely a function of the nature of regime itself: its legitimacy, and its willingness to employ extra-legal measures of persecution. The four states mentioned above are all careful not to move into the area of significant violence against Islamists.

Even where regimes themselves practice violence, as in Algeria and Egypt, the calculus to employ violence against the state must be carefully measured by the Islamists. Evidence is scant in both of these states as to whether the use of violence has intimidated the public away from potential support if the Islamists were to run in elections. Some anecdotal evidence suggests that the FIS in Algeria—at least its more militant elements—has in fact scared some of the public away, and that the FIS would fare far less well in future elections if it is permitted to run. This supposition cannot be tested until genuine open elections take place in either of these two states. It would seem logical to assume, however, that violence is a dangerous path for a political party or movement to enter, and its use will inevitably affect the party itself: it will polarize it, it will propel the more radical and violent elements to the fore, and it is then difficult for the party to retreat to a non-violent mode of action.

The third truly salient case of Islamist violence involves Hamas and the Islamic Jihad in Palestine. Conditions are different here since these movements were essentially part of a national liberation struggle against a foreign, non-Islamic power. Violence and/or terror is thus seen as partially legitimated by other Palestinians who may not fully approve the means but cannot condemn them either. The calculus shifted very significantly, however, after the PLO gained legitimacy as the negotiating partner of Israel and began to demonstrate results in working towards a peaceful settlement. At this point, not only are these two Islamist organizations weakening the peace process (as before), but they are working at direct cross purposes with the first legitimately constituted Palestinian government in the Palestinian state-to-be. They have also eschewed the opportunity to work in a legal context or to contest elections, thereby weakening their own legitimacy, except in the eyes of some extremists. Indeed, as the goals of these extremist Islamist organizations increasingly come to conflict with the daily well-being of the Palestinian masses—suffering from rough Israeli police measures, denied access to daily jobs inside Israel proper—these Islamist organizations may come to lose even greater credibility.

Perhaps some basic principle lies herein as well: Islamist movements and parties that violate the norms of legitimately constituted government and eschew legal involvement in the political process, are probably rapidly on the road to marginalization. Of course this theoretical observation is of scant comfort when we realize the tremendous power these radical Islamist organizations may have in derailing the Arab-Israeli peace process, for example, at a juncture of exceptional sensitivity. However marginal such organizations may be on the political spectrum, a small handful of activists can, at certain political junctures, wreak havoc; this is true of almost any society. But over the longer run—and this is the context in which we must view the Islamist phenomenon because it is not going to go away tomorrow—there may be some comfort in recognizing the limited basis of support such organizations will have under these circumstances.

A third key area of decision for Islamist movements is whether or not to ally with other non-Islamist parties. This is a critical issue in the "socialization" of Islamist movements, for it involves again the critical issue of compromise and operation within a legitimated political system of procedures. If Islamist parties are willing to cooperate with non-Islamist parties on a state agenda, the process of "compromise," in all its meanings, becomes operative. FIS willingness, for example, to cooperate with other Algerian parties in hammering out the Sant' Egidio proclamations against the ruling junta in Algeria in early 1995 was an important phase in the party's development, committing itself in public to a democratic process within a legal framework with certain sets of expectations. This is no certain guarantee of the future conduct of the FIS, but it is an important philosophical start. The FIS could have remained outside the Sant' Egidio framework and rejected the entire concept of elections as non-Islamic (as some in the FIS leadership in called for), but the party as a whole did not. Only time will tell how the socialization of the FIS will proceed.

Sharing of power at the parliamentary (and sometimes cabinet level) in Jordan and Kuwait has also brought Islamists into political compromise that weakens their ideological "purity" (read lack of realism). Refah participation in government at various levels in Turkey is an even more vivid example of the party tailoring its agenda to meet electoral needs. Here again then, permitting Islamists to function within a democratic framework while their party is out of power may be an important principle for future management of Islamist parties. Many parties may come to realize that they may never gain full power in a democratic order, but on the other hand they will also never be killed or jailed and will be able to represent their views indefinitely on the political spectrum.

Many fear, of course, that Islamist willingness to work within the political system today is simply a ruse to gain time, build strength, and eventually gain absolute power either through a majority victory at the ballot box or even some opportunity for a coup. Certainly, Turabi's democratic protestations in Sudan while out of power by hindsight clearly represented little more than *taqiyya* (dissembling). But hopefully the Sudanese case is not the normative model.

The final challenge to Islamist parties out of power is the question of Islamist solidarity—how to manage relations with external Islamist movements. It is not surprising that Islamist parties are in broad touch with each other. This reflects the past practice of "internationalist" Arab nationalist and Ba'th contacts. Indeed, all ideological parties will naturally consult with other like-minded groups, especially when they are banned from much activity at home. While all this can be seen as conspiratorial, it can also lend to a greater sense of shared realism. Discussion of tactics can embrace non-democratic means, but it can also include consultation on how to gain support through legitimate means. How did Islamist parties gain a sense of working at the grass roots level in the first place? Some body of shared experience must be at work here.

It is interesting to note that particular Arab states have always been nervous about any pan-Arab parties participating in the political system since these parties were often seen as the international instruments of certain regimes (the Ba'th representing Iraqi or Syrian interests, Arab nationalists representing Egypt, etc.) But in fact Islamist movements still have no "headquarters." Even the possibility of a "headquarters" would be an object of competition among Saudi Arabia, Iran, and Sudan, with no Islamist party accepting leadership or guidance from any other state or movement. This is the good news, suggesting that Islamist movements may watch each other for good ideas (and bad), but will insist on calling their own political shots within the confines of their own political orders.

These, then, represent some of the challenges and evolutionary paths in front of Islamist parties in the future. In sum, democratic means of handling them would so far seem the most successful. The nature of Islamist politics represents above all the basic political culture of the society in question, a factor usually overlooked in examining them or establishing certain expectations.

Problems of Islamism in Power

The nature of Islamist regimes in power above all reflects the means by which they came to power. Iran (power via social revolution and chaos) demonstrates the highly negative consequences of Islamists attaining full power virtually overnight, on the heels of a highly authoritarian and repressive regime, without any period of political "socialization" or governmental experience, and establishing institutions of power in the absence of any agreed rules of the game or political norms. The Sudanese experience too reflects the dangers of Islamists (or any other group) coming to power via a coup, again without subsequent restraints on their new institutions of rule. In the Sudanese case, the Islamists were not without some political experience since Turabi and others had participated to some degree in earlier regimes; the problems and demands of governance were not unknown. In Sudan, too, some kind of democratic practice had periodically existed in earlier days.

It would seem evident, then, that if regional Islamists enjoy considerable national support and power, the most auspicious and "safest" way for Islamists to attain power is within procedural frameworks that set automatic limits (in principle) to the range of their conduct. (This promises little by way of the possible wisdom of their policies.) The pessimist will argue that the Iranian and Sudanese cases so far prove the very worst about Islamist regimes—how many more do we need to get the point? The optimist might reply that the problems of the Islamists in power reflect the problems of that state's political culture in general. But one depressing conclusion may be that Islamists who gain power in the future are likely indeed to come on the heels of fairly authoritarian regimes—Egypt, Algeria, Tunisia, Saudi Arabia, Bahrain, etc. Such a situation bodes ill for the prospects that Islamists in those states will suddenly honor moderate and democratic norms that have scarcely existed under the previous regime. The major hope, then, is that these states will open up the political order to permit more moderate political evolution that in turn encourages greater adherence to new political rules on the part of the Islamists as well. "One man, one vote, one time" is not a risk limited to the Islamists but is rather a nearly universal dilemma of these states.

The argument may be raised that if authoritarianism is in the cards anyway, isn't it better to have at least "friendly" authoritarians who will pursue policies potentially less unfriendly to the West? Two alternative approaches to this question exist: focus on the immediate narrow interests of the West, or focus on the welfare and development of the state in question.

Focus on the immediate interests of the West might indicate a sensible preference for support to the "friendly" as opposed to "unfriendly" authoritarians, but only under two conditions: a belief that the Islamists (or for that matter any other unfriendly ideological party) are a distinct minority that can be marginalized by the state without serious risk; and that such perpetuation of authoritarianism will lead over time to better conditions in the future, i.e., the "authoritarian interval" will be wisely used to accomplish state and national goals that are more risky or difficult under participatory government.

To date this question cannot be clearly answered; the basis of experience is still limited. Egypt, Algeria, and Bahrain are so far hardly reassuring that the authoritarian model is effectively or wisely using its "authoritarian interval." The verdict is not yet clear in Saudi Arabia or Tunisia. But the risk of this "authoritarian option" for the West is that the end of this road offers only greater political and social explosion, making change more desirable now rather than later. This choice, of course, is not definitively in the West's hands in any case; Western policies can only partially influence the political course of events in these countries. Nor is it at all clear that the Islamists are "marginal" elements or can be marginalized via repression. Finally, does the West wish to take responsibility for the permanent delay of democratic forces in these states—values in which the West otherwise declares rhetorical belief?

Conversely, can there be any coincidence of interest between the longer term political and social welfare of these states and the interests of the West? Do we believe that democratic process may be hostile to Western interests here? The implications of such a determination are far-reaching, since democracy in almost any state then becomes questionable; U.S. protestations of belief in democracy only become a function of what serves Western interests better. This is a dangerous criterion for Western policies—and obviously short-sighted.

This paper posits that Islamist forces are here to stay and that so far no rival political movements exist in most states to challenge them—sometimes as a result of short-sighted state repression of all parties. The question then becomes one of managing the transition of Islamists into power (or partial power) in ways that will be the least destabilizing, radicalizing, or damaging to Western interests in the region as well. The first true test of whether the Islamists are inherently dedicated to ineffective, radical anti-Western policies will be their performance in power in more democratic or pluralistic institutions of governance, including the local level. Absolute power corrupts absolutely in any society including Islamist ones; absolute power for Islamists is just as undesirable in principle as it is for any party. Democratic process suggests important constitutional limits on behavior. The Refah party in Turkey, for example, so far shows no signs of playing outside the game at all, and now shares power constitutionally. Turkey may be "different," but every country is different.

Islamists faced with the problem of retaining power over the longer run also face certain challenges. It is my supposition that while Islamists ask very good questions about what is wrong with Middle Eastern governance in general, they have very few answers. (I do not rule out that Islamists in power may bring certain positive features—elimination of corruption at least initially, a sense of how to run social programs, an eye to the grass roots and people's needs, and some satisfaction of nativist impulses as opposed to internationalist ones.) But the demands for success will be overwhelming. If they begin to fail in answering the momentous questions of the day—as have most of their predecessors since the problems are truly daunting—they may rationalize that they need more time, or more power, to attain their political goals. They will be strongly tempted to turn to populism, or to accuse the opposition of underhanded tactics and destructive criticism. These are all well-known phenomena in large numbers of societies the world over. The temptation of turning to authoritarian means might then grow.

Islamists in power via democratic means will thus face the certain moment when they will be voted out of office. How will they react? A great deal will depend on the nature of the political culture that has developed—and indeed continues to develop. The tradition of democratic alternation of power takes time. Turkey is a good case in point where democratic process has gradually emerged over several decades, with the military increasingly reluctant to intervene directly. The same is true in Pakistan and Egypt, although somewhat less so. Political culture will be a key determinant.

But what of Islamists in power via non-democratic means? We have no precedents for the failure/end of such regimes (Iran and Sudan) yet. In Iran, where authoritarian ways were deeply imbedded under the Shah, the Islamic republic actually has now developed a livelier press, meaningful political parliamentary debate, and significant, honest (but not entirely free) elections, under a government far more decentralized than was the case under the Shah. This does not make the Islamic Republic of Iran any less of a problem, but it suggests avenues of evolution, and evolution today in Iran is by far the more likely scenario than revolutionary change. The regime has not been successful in most of its policies, either because the decentralized nature of power has prevented coherency of policy, or because ideology has gotten (partially) in the way—particularly in foreign policy—where the regime has been its own worst enemy.

A number of Islamist thinkers have actually tried to address the problems of alternation of power in Islamic government. A number of them (FIS, Al-Nahda, Refah) accept the idea in principle, but of course have never been put to the test. Over time, however, Islamist parties are forced to address this question in a philosophical and ideological way, i.e., do the people have the right to remove an Islamist party from power? Increasingly Islamists are reaching the conclusion that they do—since such an act will be seen as the failure of the party and not of Islam. Again, only experience will be able to validate the relevance of such Islamist political thought.

Another interesting phenomenon of Islamists in power versus those out of power touches upon the speed of evolution of many of these movements and their thinkers. This article posits that processes of evolution are palpably under way. One might offer the hypothesis that Islamists grow and mature more quickly out of power than in power, at least philosophically. It is Islamists who suffer from repression who are most mindful of what the oppressive state means; it is Islamists in exile in the West who are forced to notice aspects of Western governance in front of their eyes that bear relevance to their own states. As the premier victims of human rights violations in most states, the concept of human rights no longer becomes pure abstraction but a vital issue. Islamists out of power are forced to develop the theoretical ideas by which they challenge regimes in power; they are compelled to cast these ideas in more universal categories which are partially meaningful to Western observers, who are potential sources of sympathy. In contrast, Islamists in power are more concerned with questions of retention of power, and increasingly less with the behavior of ideal Islamist governance. How does one balance the argument that the Islamists should continue to learn by being out of power, as opposed to the argument that their exclusion only leads to greater social explosion within the state under deteriorating authoritarian rule in the future?

Future Problems Posed by Islamists

In an ideal world, Islamists, who represent a broad and serious political movement deeply grounded in native tradition and culture, should ideally be able to try their hand at governance, if supported by the majority of the public, as any other group. The West may quarrel that it prefers cultural pluralism over Islamist values, but there are few other major contenders in the political arena in the Middle East who offer this choice either. Ideally the Middle East must develop its own approach to governance and political philosophy that grows out of native (i.e. Islamic) culture—a far more solid base for future political growth than grafted or imposed Western principles. (Of course Western political principles will have major impact, but they must be organically acquired rather than imposed if they are to "take.")

The problem is that the Muslim world does not exist in a vacuum; Islamists are not fully at liberty to learn and experiment without affecting the international order. If the impact on the international order becomes too severe, they will automatically invoke Western opposition against them—as Iran and Sudan have done, as well as numerous radical Arab nationalists before them. This is international reality, and astute Islamists will come to learn the need to pursue their policies within the broader international context. Limits on radicalism inevitably exist. Islamist thinkers, leaders and movements have to decide whether they in fact seek to take on the entire international order as unjust and inequitable—which by definition any international order will be to one extent or another.

(There is little doubt in my mind that the twenty-first century will consist in any case of major challenge to the Western-dominated global order from many different quarters of the present developing world. The Islamists will be merely one among many such challengers in the arena of cultural values and imbalance of power.) But even if the Islamists are critics of the international order, how do they proceed to try to alter it? The answer to this question will have major impact on how they are perceived and treated.

So it is that Islamist regimes currently pose several serious problems to the rest of the world. The most often cited problem is that of terror. First, there should be no doubt that terror (random attacks on non-belligerent civilians) must never be condoned, by any group for whatever purpose. Political violence, usually interpreted to mean attacks on more "legitimate" targets, i.e., instruments of state power, enemy occupation, are more complex issues. The suicide bombings in Israel in March 1996 were especially terrible, not just for the loss of life—always a tragedy anywhere—but for the ability of a fringe group to have destabilized and fundamentally altered the highly delicate peace process at a crucial juncture. Never has political violence and terror in the modern Middle East had such potentially fateful consequences in being able to derail and destroy carefully built edifices enjoying majority support.

Islamist movements of course have no monopoly on terror or political violence—some of the worst of it in past decades was secular and nationalist, and still remains so among Palestinian leftist groups. Apart from the fateful terrorist acts in Israel in March 1996, most of the violence and terror has been directed against local regimes rather than against outside powers. (Another spectacular exception was the World Trade Center bombing in New York.) Iranian terrorism has been primarily directed against its own domestic enemies abroad. Iranian support to Hizbullah in Lebanon—a radical and unattractive group, but still arguably engaged in guerrilla attacks against Israeli occupation forces—has been highly effective with international overtones. A further objectionable feature of both the Iranian and Sudanese regimes—especially to Middle Eastern rulers—is their willingness to grant refuge to Islamist activists wanted in their own countries. However, a large number of these individuals are not necessarily criminals, but are simply political refugees. Some indeed are granted asylum in Western countries (Muhammad al-Mas'ari from Saudi Arabia in London, Rashid al-Ghannushi from Tunisia in London, Anwar Haddam from Algeria in Washington, etc.) Others in fact may be fugitives from the law for specific violent acts.

The single greatest dilemma in dealing with "Islamist terrorism" in the future is the indiscriminate use of this term to cover a wide variety of problems. Islamist violence is quite real, but is regularly politicized by local regimes as well as Western governments to different ends. Governments will make their political pronouncements to serve their own policy ends; thus states like Egypt, Algeria, Tunisia, and Uzbekistan all find it useful to smear all political opposition with the label of terrorist, and indeed often seek to goad opposition into such acts so that they can be eliminated without further explanation to the West.

But more serious and objective observers need to note the variety of types of action that require different responses. Are Iran and Sudan actually the main source of political terrorism and violence in the region? One of the few legitimate litmus tests that can be applied to this problem is whether the major problem at hand would go away if Iran or Sudan ceased to exist. Unless the answer to this is yes, then these regimes are not the main source of the problem but mainly represent exacerbating factors. (Even exacerbating factors may have had fateful political impact in Israel in March 1996—a stunning exception.) That these Islamist regimes are undesirable is unquestionable, since they do not facilitate the conduct of international relations. The question is the efficacy of policy response. The West still seeks in vain effective means of dealing with either Iran or Sudan, but has shortsightedly chosen to single them out for total repudiation and isolation while demonstrating willingness to show greater balance, pragmatism and measured response towards other "rogue regimes" such as Syria, China and North Korea. Domestic politicization of these issues in both Washington and Israel has further complicated the problem. Are we convinced that isolation and demonization will prove effective instruments against Islamist terrorism and political violence in the future?

The greatest danger to the future of the Middle East may now lie in the looming convergence between authoritarian regimes—who perpetuate their power and incompetence on the rationale of struggle against terror—and Western governments that find their rationale useful. For the first time, the West may now be swinging behind de facto adoption of anti-democratic policies out of fear of elections (that elect Islamists), change in the regional status quo, or a single-minded fixation upon "terror" (however minimal in the greater order of international conflict)—to the neglect of all else.

Terror is the ideal proxy target, distracting from the extremely complex political and social problems this paper has tried to set forth. The sad reality is that change in the regional status quo—political, economic, and social—is long overdue and will come; the longer it is delayed, the more convulsive it is likely to be. Political Islam may now have provided the ideological justification for the West to turn its back on its own professed political ideals in the name of the struggle against terror and a preference for the status quo shared with bad governance in the region.

Islamist movements thus lie at the center of this major ideological struggle in the next century. Regional regimes and Western policymakers find themselves at fateful crossroads. The next century in the Middle East will not be stable under any circumstances, given the nature of long overdue change. Large portions of the world will push for greater democratization, social and economic justice, and a more equitable balance of power in the world. The Islamists will be among them, for better or for worse. How difficult will the West make that process that so clearly lies ahead? Future Western policies towards Islamist movements and regimes hold the key to the answer.

The Mismeasure of Political Islam

Martin Kramer

Perhaps no development of the last decade of the twentieth century has caused as much confusion in the West as the emergence of political Islam. Just what does it portend? Is it against modernity, or is it an effect of modernity? Is it against nationalism, or is it a form of nationalism? Is it a striving for freedom, or a revolt against freedom?

One would think that these are difficult questions to answer, and that they would inspire deep debates. Yet over the past few years, a surprisingly broad consensus has emerged within academe about the way political Islam should be measured. This consensus has begun to spread into parts of government as well, especially in the U.S. and Europe. A paradigm has been built, and its builders claim that its reliability and validity are beyond question.

This now-dominant paradigm runs as follows. The Arab Middle East and North Africa are stirring. The peoples in these lands are still under varieties of authoritarian or despotic rule. But they are moved by the same universal yearning for democracy which transformed Eastern Europe and Latin America. True, there are no movements we would easily recognize as democracy movements. But for historical and cultural reasons, this universal yearning has taken the form of Islamist protest movements. If these do not look like democracy movements, that is only a consequence of our own age-old bias against Islam. When the veil of prejudice is lifted, one will see Islamist movements for what they are: the functional equivalents of democratic reform movements.

True, on the edges of these movements are groups that are atavistic and authoritarian. Some of their members are prone to violence. These are the "extremists." But the mainstream movements are essentially open, pluralistic, and nonviolent, led by "moderates" or "reformists." These "moderates" can be strengthened if they are made partners in the political process, and an initial step must be dialogue. But ultimately the most

Martin Kramer is director of the Moshe Dayan Center for Middle Eastern and African Studies, Tel Aviv University.

effective way to domesticate the Islamists is to permit them to share or possess power. There is no threat here unless the West creates it, by supporting acts of state repression that would deny Islamists access to participation or power.

There are several hidden assumptions beneath this paradigm:

• First, that the yearning for democracy is today universal, and stands behind the mass Islamist movements.

• Second, that there are "extremists" and "moderates" in Islamist movements, and that they can be reliably identified, classified, and separated, both for analytical and policy purposes.

• Third, that power has a moderating effect upon those who share or exercise it, and would have such an effect upon Islamists as well.

• Fourth, that because Islamism represents the populist will, its triumph is inevitable.

These assumptions form the four legs of the paradigmatic table. Take one out, and the paradigm collapses. Do any of these legs wobble? Perhaps all four do.

Universal Democrats

The first assumption holds that the yearning for democracy is today universal, and stands behind the mainstream Islamist movements.

Looking at the dismal state of government across the expanse of Islam, many observers conclude that all broad-based opposition can have only one purpose: democratic reform. One political scientist assures us that "the Islamist movements are basically social reform movements,"[1] another expert tells us these are "political reform movements."[2] Still another political scientist, a bit more cautious, tells a congressional committee that "whatever the ultimate intent of Islamist movements, their current function is a liberalizing one."[3] The dominant analogy is to the parties of "reform" in the former Soviet bloc. This is the age of democracy triumphant. It is a free good desired by everyone.

But is it? The other powerful mobilizing force unleashed by the break-up of the Soviet bloc has been the dormant creature called nationalism. In places like the former Yugoslavia, a nationalist surge brought genocide back to Europe. Elsewhere, especially in the former Soviet Union where the democratic tradition is weak, the forces of nationalism are rallying. The first priority of these movements is authenticity, and their position vis-à-vis pluralism, both social and political, is ambivalent at best. In the past few years, political scientists have scrambled to cobble together some understanding of why nationalism returns.

Has it occurred to the paradigm builders that the return of nationalism might provide a more telling analogy for Islamist movements? It is generally agreed that Islamism arose from the failure of Arab (and Iranian and Turkish) nationalism. Not only is this obvious; one might go further: Islamism represents a remake of nationalism as Islamic ideology. Nationalism, leavened by religion, thus becomes a hyper-nationalism. Said Arjomand, sociologist of Iran's revolution, has looked closely at this possibility, and locates the closest analogy to today's Islamist movements in the Rumanian Iron Guards, who combined religious fervor with nationalist chauvinism.[4]

If mainstream Islamist discourse on democracy, minorities, foreigners, women, and cosmopolitan intellectuals, sounds ominously familiar, it is because identical words emanate from the nationalist right in Europe. By any reading, this discourse evokes not Havel and Walesa, but Le Pen and Zhirinovsky. Listen to Hasan al-Turabi of the Sudan, the Sorbonne-schooled ideologue of Islamism: "You talk about freedom, so that the people can express its will. Profess freedom without national liberation and the imperialist will intervene and falsify your will. Elections will express *his* will, the political party will be *his* agent, the newspaper will be *his* mouthpiece."[5] This is a classic nationalist argument, with a slight fascist overtone that has become the stock-in-trade of the Sudanese oracle.

But Turabi puts its precisely: Islamist movements are first of all about national liberation, not individual liberties; they are about power before politics; their populism is a form of mass mobilization, not participation. It is not the yearning for democracy that drives these movements. It is the yearning for authenticity, by people who are aggrieved and angry, and vulnerable to Islamist promises of power and revenge. There is a debate among Islamists about democracy, and it is useful to follow it. But it is a circular debate over whether democracy is or is not authentically Islamic. By Islamist consensus, however, democracy is not a value in its own right; and the very fact that a democratic outcome is debated, and not assumed, is the sign of a profound ambivalence.

The fact that some Islamist movements are mass movements is not, ipso facto, a democratic or liberal credential. To call them "liberalizing" because they oppose illiberal regimes assumes a great deal. Is it possible that any people would prefer authenticity to democracy? It is more than possible: it has happened repeatedly across Europe, Asia, and Africa. This is the lesson of nationalism's temptation, perhaps the costliest learned in this century. There are of course people in the Middle East and North Africa who do yearn for democracy. Not surprisingly, they include many of Islamism's most vocal critics—and many of its victims.

"Extremists" and "Moderates"

The second assumption holds that there are "extremists" and "moderates" in Islamist movements, who can be reliably identified, classified, and separated.

Obviously there must be differences among Islamists. A scholar has repeatedly urged that the U.S. government "distinguish between Islamic movements that are a threat and those that represent legitimate indigenous attempts to reform and redirect their societies."[6] This seems an eminently reasonable objective on paper, but in practice it means going out, measuring each movement, and classifying it. What instrument of measurement do we use, and what do we measure?

One might immediately say, why not do content analysis of what Islamists say? These are blueprints; perhaps we should read them? But the paradigm builders resist this, especially when those texts threaten violence. One political scientist warns that knowing "who the Islamist groups are and what they are doing" is impossible if the West "is preoccupied with content analysis of the Islamists' frequently contradictory statements."[7] Content analysis is denounced as "new Orientalism," a preoccupation with texts that have nothing to do with what Islamists are truly about. Whatever violence the Islamists deploy in speech or print, this must not be allowed to disqualify them from potential classification as "moderates." One must go out and watch them. And it must be admitted that the paradigm builders can never be accused of misreading political Islam; to misread, one must first read, and this they adamantly refuse to do.

But when one begins to watch "what [the Islamists] are doing," other paradigm builders proclaim that this is no reliable guide either, especially when it is violence that is on display. A political scientist has explained to a U.S. congressional committee his own system of classification, which employs the acronym "NINA"—"Nonviolent Islamists in North Africa." These are defined as "moderate" advocates of the "non-violent transfer of political power." Now as it turns out, Islamists do not have to *practice* non-violence to qualify for "NINA" status. Even when they "degenerate" into violence, determines this political scientist, violence "does not constitute a structural component of either their strategic thinking or tactical actions."[8] And so they remain "non-violent" "moderates" however many bombs they set off and intellectuals they kill—since they don't *tell* us explicitly why they are doing it. To know their minds, we are sent running back to the texts, looking for thought structures—like "new Orientalists."

In the end, the paradigm builders are profoundly indifferent to what Islamists say or do. To know the paradigm itself is to know what the Islamists are, and what they must become. It is a privileged tool of divination, allowing only its masters to separate the real "extremists" from the real "moderates." Not surprisingly, given this disdain for what normally constitutes evidence, many believers in the paradigm are prepared to declare all the major Islamist movements and their offshoots to be essentially or potentially "moderate," even when they say violence and make violence. The paradigm builders, having promised to make useful distinctions, end up making none whatsoever.

If there is anything more simplistic than lumping Islamists together, it has been the attempt to divide them into the neat categories of "reformist" and "extremist." William Zartman has pointed to "the usual division of Islamic parties into a moderate, usually visible leadership and a radical militant wing, often underground."[9] If this is the usual division, then how does one classify an Islamic movement which is simultaneously a political group, a militia, and an amalgam of terror cells? How does one classify a formation which seeks recognition as a political party even as it sets off car bombs in public streets? The murky combination of political party, armed militia, and terror cell is hardly the usual constitution of a "reform" movement, and is virtually impossible to classify along simple lines.

The U.S. has tried to draw these distinctions, with predictable results: America's past Islamist partners in dialogue are today imprisoned in the U.S. for terrorism, listed as terrorists by the State Department, or virtually banned from entry as undesirables. The search for the "moderates," who exist in theory, continues; U.S. diplomats meet with Islamists in Egypt, Jordan, Lebanon, Turkey. But can these diplomats reliably separate, classify, and categorize the Islamists on their beats? Leaving the question of diplomatic competence aside, the task is an impossible one, because these categories are paradigmatic ideal types, not existing realities.

"Power Moderates"

The third assumption holds that power has a moderating effect upon those who share or exercise it. This is probably the most cherished axiom in the paradigm, since it promises that even "extremists" can be redeemed and rehabilitated. Even if it is allowed that Islamist movements are not yet movements of "reform," perhaps they themselves can be reformed?

That will only happen, it is argued, if the Islamists are allowed to compete openly for power. Here is an intelligence analyst-turned-political scientist: "Democracy is probably the best road by which to seek the moderation of radically minded Islamist parties. Islamists are forced toward greater moderation and acceptance of democratic processes when they are required to compete in open elections."[10] And after elections, writes this same analyst, "Islamists will inevitably be forced to compromise with political reality as they move into positions of authority within parliaments and have to deal with those they do not agree with."[11]

The logical extension of this argument is that absolute power "moderates" absolutely—that if you really want "moderate" Islamists, you should not only wish them to share power, but to have it in spades. And indeed, one journalist has even argued that the U.S. "must not only allow but actively encourage Islamists to come to power by democratic means and experiment with ways that blend political pluralism and Islam."[12]

There are at least two obvious problems with this assumption: the two extant examples of Islamism in power, Iran and Sudan. The results of these two "experiments" fill the reports of human rights organizations and terrorism monitoring agencies, and pose what might seem an insurmountable problem for the formula that "power moderates." And so the paradigm builders must explain Iran and Sudan—or, more precisely, explain them away.

This has been done in different ways, but the most interesting approach was taken by a political scientist before a congressional committee:

> Since the only Islamist Governments in power today obtained their position by coup [i.e., Sudan] or revolution [i.e., Iran], we do not, in fact, have a precedent from which to predict the behavior of popularly elected Islamist Governments. We do know that no revolution or military coup has produced democratic government; what we do not know is whether popularly elected Islamists will be willing or able to sustain democracy.[13]

In other words, Iran and Sudan are not valid results for the experiment at hand, because the Islamists were somehow ruined by the way they acquired power. The argument here is that power is exercised in the way it is acquired, and not in the way it is conceived.

Can this be anything but an article of blind faith? The exceptions are as large as modern history. American democracy came to power through insurrection and revolution. Nazi dictatorship took power through the ballot. (Lord Bullock, Hitler's biographer, described the Nazi case as one of "revolution after power.") When the question is whether power will be used or abused, ideas about power have been better predictors than the way in which it has been acquired. In this respect, Iran and Sudan are arguably exemplary of Islamism in power. One is Sunni, the other is Shiite; one is African and Arab, the other is Asian and Persian; one is resource-poor, one is resource-rich; and yet the results are more or less the same.

Indeed, wherever there are faint signs of Islamist "moderation," it would seem to correlate with greater distance from power. If one were to name the three leading Islamist leaders and thinkers today, one would probably settle on three men: Rashid al-Ghannushi of Tunisia, Muhammad Husayn Fadlallah of Lebanon's Hizbullah, and Hasan al-Turabi of Sudan. Each also stands in a different relationship to power. Ghannushi is in exile, as distant from power as he can be. Fadlallah is the leader of a movement in Lebanon which is a functioning political party, perhaps somewhere on the road to power. Turabi is in power.

If they are compared, say, on the crucial issue of political pluralism, there are significant variations in their positions. But the correlation is the *opposite* of that posited by the paradigm. Ghannushi, who is the furthest from power, at least professes acceptance of full multiparty democracy. Fadlallah, who stands in an intermediate position, advocates a strictly Islamic multiparty system—limited to Islamic parties alone. Turabi calls any party system divisive; he advocates a no-party system, governed almost secretly in the name of Islam, with the unfortunate results now evident in Sudan.

In short, power, rather than "moderate," would seem to lead Islamists to make ever more elaborate rationales for denying it to others. A far more sustainable assumption would be this: Islamists, who are rational people, "moderate" when they face overwhelming counter-power. But the more power they themselves possess, the more faithfully they revert to their core agenda, dominated by elements most in the West would regard as "extreme."

All the evidence is that power does not "moderate." Weakness "moderates." Islamists have been "tamed," coopted into political systems, only when it has been absolutely clear to them that the rules preclude them from acquiring a monopoly of power. That is why co-optation has worked in monarchies like Jordan and Kuwait, and in Turkey and Syrian-run Lebanon—and why it has been a formula for deepening conflict elsewhere.

Inevitable Islamism

The fourth and last assumption holds that because Islamism represents the populist will, its triumph is inevitable. After the outbreak of the Algerian civil war, many experts argued that the triumph of Islamic movements in the Arab world could not be prevented. The Arab expanse, they said, was like Eastern Europe: a set of dominoes, set to fall before Islamic movements. Algeria would go first—its fall to the Islamists was predicted with confidence. (Six months after the Algerian coup, a leading journalist wrote in *Foreign Affairs* that it was "in many ways like the abortive Moscow putsch in 1991; although the process may take longer, it will fail for similar reasons.")[14]

Yet eighteen years after Iran's revolution, and five years after the war began in Algeria, there has been no second Islamic revolution. Despite the violence, the regimes are still in place. The men who have ruled the Middle East and North Africa for a generation still rule it today. Algeria is still a place of violent confrontation, but the regime has held its ground, and even held presidential elections that demonstrated impressive support for its president—despite an Islamist boycott of elections. More recently, an overwhelming majority of Algerian voters approved a new constitution excluding Islamists from power.

What is true about Algeria is even more true about Egypt. Four years ago, there were experts who warned that Egypt could go Islamist; terrorism replaced tourism. Today the most violent Islamists have been pushed back into the most remote part of Egypt. Many languish in prison; the Muslim Brothers are crying foul, but also crying uncle; and the tourists are coming back. In other places in the Arab world, there are manifestations of Islamist opposition and violence, but nowhere are they regime-threatening.

Where did so many of the experts go wrong? Above all, they underestimated the power of the state. The lesson of the Iranian revolution was not that Islamic movements were all-powerful. It was that rulers could fall if they showed weakness. The Shah, despite his omnipotent image, had become a weak ruler. He had been diminished by his cancer, he thought America had abandoned him.

But this did not mean other rulers would show the same weakness, or repeat the Shah's mistakes. And they have not. They have understood that the preservation of their power is tantamount to their physical survival. Faced with Islamist opposition, they have fought back. They have used their intelligence apparatus and security forces, their courts and their prisons. It has not been done in accord with Western notions of human rights or democracy. But the sum of it is that every Arab ruler threatened by an Islamist opposition has found a way to contain it or confront it—

from Syria's Hafiz Asad to Iraq's Saddam Husayn, from Tunisia's Ben Ali to Egypt's Husni Mubarak. The newest addition to this club is Yasir Arafat, elected leader of the Palestinian Authority.

Repression is working. It is a tired academic sawhorse that repression only strengthens its victims. Islamic history is strewn with dissident groups and revolutionary sects that were repressed out of existence. In the Arab Middle East, the state is still stronger than society, civil or otherwise. This is why there are no revolutions—and also why there is no democracy. Those Islamists who understand the state's abiding strength, who now bend in the wind, are likely to survive to fight another day. The others seem bound to be extinguished.

Nor should one underestimate the impact of the mistakes and weaknesses of the Islamists themselves. For an Islamist movement to make a bid for power, Islamists need secular allies—others who are not Islamists, but who are prepared to join them against the rulers. Here lies one of the fundamental flaws of the Islamists. They cannot tolerate those who differ with them, certainly not long enough to obtain power. Impatient for that power, they begin to purge society even before they rule, with disastrous results for themselves.

This occurred in Algeria, where Islamists embarked on a campaign of killing intellectuals, blowing up journalists, and slitting the throats of unveiled women. Whole segments of society learned to fear the Islamists more than the regime. If the government has an upper hand today, this is largely because of the egregious mistakes of the Islamists in reading the response of the Algerian people. The same occurred also in Egypt, where the Islamist targeting of tourism undermined the millions of individual Egyptian households that depend on tourism for their livelihoods. It was broader Egyptian society that was harmed by the Islamist violence—and it was broader Egyptian society that turned against the Islamists.

"All movements go too far," said Bertrand Russel. The Islamists went too far, and now are paying for it dearly. Not only did the West's experts prophesy falsely when they predicted an Islamist triumph. They failed to anticipate the deep crisis which now afflicts the Islamists, and which in some countries could augur their demise.

The Collapse of a Paradigm

In sum, the dominant paradigm has failed. It has mistaken virulent forms of hyper-nationalism for social and political reformism. It has misleadingly classified Islamist movements into "moderate" and "extreme" categories that do not exist. It has made hopelessly naive assumption about the effect of power on Islamist behavior. And it has postulated the inevitable triumph of a movement which is now in the throes of a crisis. Why is there so much support for a paradigm which so utterly fails to describe or predict?

The most important factor is the predispositions of contemporary academe. For most academic commentators on things Islamic, 1978 is a watershed—not because a stern Shiite cleric inspired a revolution, but because a stern Columbia literature professor published a book. Edward Said's *Orientalism* persuaded them that their only legitimate role was to apologize and sympathize. Today it is difficult to find a scholarly discourse more self-conscious than the scholarly discourse on political Islam. Indeed, many practitioners have only one eye on the movements they purport to study. The other eye is fixed squarely on disciplinary dogma, which holds that any feverish act done in the name of Islam should be shown a respectful deference—repentance for historic wrongs done by the West against Muslims. This has been a major obstacle not only to understanding, but to open debate itself.

The area experts have been joined by well-intentioned political scientists, schooled in the optimism of American liberalism, who are certain everyone really wants to enjoy what the West enjoys, in the way the West enjoys it. In a paradoxical way, theirs is the ultimate ethnocentrism. It posits universal values and universal motives, which in the end turn out to be precisely our own. But the world is an infinitely varied place, and many of its people are struggling with a sense of grievance and desire for revenge difficult for others to imagine. This is nowhere more true than in the case of political Islam.

The dominant paradigm, then, is defective, and those who continue to employ it will continue to mismeasure political Islam, with more and more damaging results. If the paradigm is broken, what is to be done? Clearly, there is a need for an alternative paradigm. It should realistically see political Islam as part of the global resurgence of nationalism. It should throw out meaningless, static categories, and instead try to map the interconnections between the volatile components of political Islam. It should face head-on the serious complications that arise when political Islam achieves political power. And it should take into account the strength of the state, and the evident tendency of Islamists to alienate potential allies. Far fewer minds are at work on this alternative paradigm, but its power is not in numbers, and it has already opened space for debate.

And political Islam must continue to be debated. One hears a great deal about the need for dialogue. But in the present climate, there seems to be a far greater need for vigorous debate. A few years back, a political scientist, in an appearance before a committee of congress, urged that the U.S. "find ways of engaging Islamist politicians in dialogue that will emphasize our commonalities, not our differences."[15] There could be no greater guarantee of misunderstanding. The differences are real, and they will not vanish simply because they are skirted. But if they are debated openly in the West, then this is sure to give courage to others, in the Middle East and North Africa. Such debate may even fan the embers of a more far-reaching transformation in Islam itself.

NOTES

1. Augustus Richard Norton, "Breaking through the Wall of Fear in the Arab World," *Current History* (January 1992): 41.
2. John Esposito quoted in *Islam and Democracy: Religion, Politics, and Power in the Middle East*, ed. Timothy D. Sisk (Washington: United States Institute of Peace, 1992), 12-13.
3. Statement by Michael C. Hudson, House Committee on Foreign Affairs, Subcommittee on Europe and the Middle East, *Promoting Pluralism and Democracy in the Middle East*, 102d Congress, 2d sess., 11 August 1992, 36.
4. Said Amir Arjomand, *The Turban for the Crown: The Islamic Revolution in Iran* (New York: Oxford University Press, 1988), 209.
5. Speech by Turabi to the Popular Arab-Islamic Conference, *Al-Islam wa-Filastin* (Nicosia), May-June 1991.
6. John Esposito quoted in *Islam and Democracy*, 12-13.
7. Ghassan Salamé, "Islam and the West," *Foreign Policy*, no. 90 (Spring 1993): 32.

8. Statement by John Entelis, House Committee on Foreign Affairs, Subcommittee on Africa, *Recent Developments in North Africa,* 103d Congress, 2d sess., 28 September 1994.

9. I. William Zartman, "Democracy and Islam: The Cultural Dialectic," in *Political Islam,* eds. Charles E. Butterworth and I. William Zartman (=*Annals of the American Academy of Political and Social Scien*ce, no. 524 [November 1992]): 189. This was precisely Zartman's view of Algeria's Islamic Salvation Front, whose "moderates" were "simply front-men" for a "militant leadership." See interview with Zartman, *Middle East Affairs* (Spring-Summer 1993): 59.

10. Graham Fuller, *Islamic Fundamentalism in the Northern Tier Countries: An Integrative View* (Santa Monica, California: RAND Corporation, 1991), xii, 21.

11. Graham Fuller, "A Phased Introduction of Islamists," in *Democracy in the Middle East,* 25.

12. Robin Wright, "U.S. Needs Foreign Policy on Islam," *Los Angeles Times,* 7 July 1993.

13. Testimony by Lisa Anderson, in House Committee, *Promoting Pluralism,* 5.

14. Robin Wright, "Islam, Democracy and the West," *Foreign Affairs* 71, no. 3 (Summer 1992): 136.

15. Hearing statement by Michael C. Hudson, in House Committee, *Promoting Pluralism,* 37-38.

Index